THE
SHORESAVER'S
HANDBOOK

THE
SHORESAVER'S
HANDBOOK

AN AMERICAN LITTORAL
SOCIETY BOOK

TUCKER COOMBE

LYONS & BURFORD, PUBLISHERS

Printed in the United States of America

Design by Catherine Lau Hunt

10 9 8 7 6 5 4 3 2 1

Library of Congress Cataloging-in-Publication Data

Coombe, Tucker.
    The shoresaver's handbook / Tucker Coombe.
        p.   cm.
    "An American Littoral Society book."
    Includes bibliographical references and index.
    ISBN 1-55821-401-1
    1. Marine pollution.   2. Coastal zone management.
  I. Title.
GC1085.C668   1996
333.91'716—dc20   96-13075
                                             CIP

CONTENTS

Introduction

The more one learns about coastal pollution, the easier it is to become overwhelmed, to turn and walk away from the problem. The effects of polluted waters can be felt everywhere. Vast expanses of sea grass, which serve as vital breeding, feeding, and nursery grounds for everything from barnacles to waterfowl, have disappeared from some of the nation's estuaries. More than a third of the country's shellfish beds have been contaminated by raw sewage, and each year, thousands of beaches are declared unsafe for swimming.

Marine debris is every bit as pervasive as polluted waters. The problem can be seen not only along American beaches, where once-pristine expanses of sand are now dotted with rusty metal cans, plastic water jugs, pieces of fishing net, twisted ropes of plastic sheeting, and a profusion of cigarette butts, but also in regions as remote as Antarctica, where so much debris washes up each year that conservationists are considering initiating an annual cleanup along its shores. For marine and coastal wildlife, the impact of this debris is far more than aesthetic. Significant numbers of the sea turtles that wash up dead along the shores of the southeastern United States are discovered to have ingested items such as balloons, foamed plastic "peanuts," and plastic bags. Nearly half of the world's species of seals have been found entangled in items such as fishing nets and plastic strapping bands. Sperm whale carcasses, examined at a whaling station in Iceland, have been found to contain plastic drinking cups, fishing nets, and children's toys.

For some, the degradation of the coastal and marine environment has served as a sort of call to arms. These people are combing the beach for debris, even descending to the underwater realm to gather discarded hooks, lead sinkers, and fishing line, all as part of a massive coastal cleanup. They are testing surfing waters for bacterial contamination, identifying pollution "hot spots," and turning up at town meetings to fight against damaging coastal development. Some are patrolling beaches to keep them safe for nesting sea turtles, while others are rehabilitating entangled shorebirds.

This handbook aims to show the scope, the strength, and the potential of this sort of coastal conservation. It is my hope that the book will spawn some new thoughts on how to restore the health of local estuaries and coastal regions, and—for those considering initiating projects in their own communities, or linking up with projects already under way—provide plenty of information on where to turn for guidance and further advice. Certain subjects, important as they are to coastal conservation, lie outside the scope of the book. For this reason, shoreline erosion, dunes, and beach restoration are not discussed in these pages.

Chapter 1 deals with the pervasive threat of marine debris, with particular attention given to the deadly role of plastics, and looks at how citizens are cleaning up coastal regions and targeting debris at its sources. Chapter 2 examines the many organizations and individuals fighting the insidious and often invisible scourge of polluted waters. Chapter 3 looks at those most at risk from contaminated, debris-strewn waters—the animals that share our shores and inhabit the world's oceans—and identifies the people who are working on behalf of these creatures. The final chapter offers dozens and dozens of simple, straightforward suggestions—covering subjects from water conservation to environmentally sound shopping—for those interested in restoring the well-being of our waters.

The Threat of Debris

Oceans—vast, powerful, and seemingly fathomless—have long been perceived as having an infinite ability to absorb human refuse. And for centuries, debris has been flung by the ton into their depths—garbage, tossed off the end of a pier; raw sewage, piped directly into a harbor; rotten food, cloth and wood objects, even corpses, all routinely hoisted over the sides of ships. But because all of these materials, sooner or later, decomposed, the oceans remained fairly healthy in the face of this treatment. Today, however, garbage that finds its way into the oceans is not nearly so benign; and clearly, oceans and their inhabitants are suffering under the onslaught. Each year, for example, thousands of marine animals die by ingesting or becoming entangled in human refuse. The most deadly form of this refuse, moreover, happens to be that which is most prevalent: plastics.

In the past few decades plastics have established a strong, ubiquitous presence in our lives. Consider that in 1960, approximately 6.3 billion pounds of plastics were produced in the United States; by 1993, the figure had soared to 68.8 billion. Because trash-disposal practices, for many, still reflect the mentality of centuries past, vast quantities of plastics inevitably wind up in the marine environment.

Plastic marine debris can be divided into two types: easily identifiable objects, many of them (six-pack rings, plastic bags, shrink-wrap, and bottles, for example) representing packaging materials; and plastic resin pellets, small beads about the size of a match head,which serve as the raw material for these products. Plastic objects follow numerous paths to the marine environment; plastic pellets, on the other hand, usually wind up in the ocean as a result of sloppy handling during manufacturing or transport.

THE PARTICULAR PERILS OF PLASTIC

Plastics are strong, lightweight, and durable, qualities that make them not only indispensible in our daily lives, but deadly to those living in the ocean. Because they are lightweight, plastics tend to float, thereby enticing marine animals that mistake them for natural food. Plastic bags and sheeting, for example, are often consumed by sea turtles that confuse them with jellyfish. Plastic pellets resemble floating fish and crab eggs, and are routinely eaten by seabirds and fish. Marine creatures such as squid may congregate around floating debris, and when they are consumed by larger animals, so, too, is the debris.

Plastics are also extremely strong, and when an animal becomes entangled in plastic netting or line and struggles to break free, it is usually a futile endeavor. Evidence of this can be seen in Florida, where each year hundreds of pelicans become entangled in monofilament fishing line and wind up dangling from tree limbs in their own rookeries, starved or strangled to death. An equally tragic situation occurs when seal pups begin playing with discarded plastic strapping bands (used to bind pallets on cargo ships) or fragments of fishing nets. After the plastic becomes lodged around the animal's neck or flipper, it simply tightens as the animal grows, with strangulation or fatal laceration the ultimate result. And finally, because plastic objects are so durable, they remain intact for decades, possibly centuries, in the marine environment. Plastic fishing nets, long after being lost or abandoned at sea, continue to "ghost fish," ensnaring and killing fish, birds, and any other marine animals that encounter them. A single net can do tremendous damage: One nine-mile-long gill net, found floating off the coast of Alaska, was discovered to have caught 350 seabirds as well as hundreds of valuable salmon.

Given the prevalence of marine debris, perhaps it is no wonder that many animals come in contact with plastics. Researchers who perform necropsies (animal autopsies) on stranded sea turtles report finding plastic in the stomachs of between one-third and one-half of all the animals they examine. And in a 1982 study of the North Pacific fur seal population, researchers concluded that approximately fifty thousand seals died annually from entanglement in marine debris, most of it plastic fishing nets and strapping bands. (Fortunately, the number is believed to have declined since then.) For marine species with stable populations, the impact of plastics may not ultimately play a role in any species' long-term viability. But for rare or endangered species, such as the Hawaiian monk seal, plastics are just one more threat to species survival.

Animals, of course, are not alone in finding debris a problem. Discarded monofilament line can easily get wrapped around boat propellers. Plastic bags can clog boat intake valves. Broken glass and half-buried, rusty pop cans can slice open the foot of a child walking along a beach. And at an aesthetic level, debris is just plain ugly. People vacation at the shore to relax, take long walks along the beach, swim, fish, and enjoy local scenery; but if the local scenery includes gallon jugs, motor oil containers, and segments of plastic rope that float in with each tide, visitors may opt to spend their next vacation elsewhere. And although it may be impossible to put a monetary value on a clean beach, experts have on occasion gauged the price of a dirty one: When medical waste washed ashore on the coasts of New York and New Jersey during the summers of 1987 and 1988, the incidents received such publicity that visitors decided to stay away, which cost the two states almost two billion dollars in lost revenue.

WHERE IT ALL COMES FROM

For those who have walked along the beach and noted the tremendous variety of debris washed up on the sand, half hidden in the eelgrass, or enmeshed in dried seaweed, often the question that comes to mind is: How in the world did *that* get there? The Center for Marine Conservation (CMC), the organization in the United States that perhaps more than any other has made its business one of studying marine debris, has pinpointed the likely sources of many types of debris. In broad terms, debris can usually be classified as either "land-based" or "ocean-based."

Land-based Sources

"Urban means city, city means people, and people mean

trash," writes Kathy Hart of North Carolina Sea Grant. "Add an adjacent ocean to the equation, and trash means marine debris." When one considers that some 70 percent of the United States population lives within fifty miles of a coast (including the Great Lakes), it is no surprise that the bulk of marine debris comes from land-based sources. Here are some of them.

Storm-drain Systems: Storm drains, designed to carry rainwater off city streets, also carry anything that can fit through the grate of a storm drain or the opening of a storm sewer, and deposit it, usually unfiltered and untreated, in a nearby waterway. Candy wrappers, cigarette butts, plastic straws and drink lids, Styrofoam cups, and plastic bags all find their way to coastal waters this way. "Throw it on the ground today, and you'll be swimming with it tomorrow," says Roger Gorke, of the coastal conservation group Heal the Bay in Santa Monica, California.

Combined Sewer Systems: When beach litter includes tampon applicators, condoms, and syringes, it is a good bet that combined sewer systems are the culprit. In these systems, storm-drain runoff is combined with residential sewage and funneled to a sewage treatment plant. But when the system is overburdened by heavy rains, everything, including raw sewage and the debris that travels with it, is piped directly to the nearest waterway (see the discussion of "Urbanization," chapter 2). A 1989–91 survey carried out in New York Harbor found that 85 percent of the harbor's floating debris came from storm drains and combined sewer overflows.

Beachgoers: Items often associated with beach litter include six-pack rings, pop cans and bottles, cigarette butts, plastic sandwich bags, fireworks, and suntan lotion bottles. And debris of this sort adds up: The Los Angeles County Department of Beaches and Harbors reports that during the Labor Day weekend of 1995, beachgoers covering a thirty-one-mile stretch of beach produced some fifty tons of debris.

Ocean-based Sources

Following are a few of the culprits believed responsible for much of the world's ocean dumping.

Merchant Shipping: Ships carrying cargo tend to use plastic, because of its light weight and strength, to package everything from galley supplies to transported cargo. Plastic strapping bands, sheeting, and shrink-wrap, all associated with merchant vessels, take a terrible toll on wildlife.

Offshore Petroleum Activities: The types of debris often associated with oil and gas platforms include plastic hard hats, wooden spools, wooden pallets, fifty-five-gallon drums, and Styrofoam buoys. Debris of this type is especially prevalent along the Gulf of Mexico.

Recreational Fishing: One of the deadliest forms of debris imaginable is monofilament line, which fishermen often cut when it becomes snarled or snagged on an object. It is not unusual to find a single segment of line with several dead birds entangled in it.

OCEAN DUMPING: WHAT'S LEGAL, WHAT'S NOT, AND WHAT HAPPENS ANYWAY

No matter how prevalent it may be, the vast majority of ocean dumping is nonetheless illegal. Since the late 1980s the

United States has been part of an international agreement, known informally as the MARPOL Protocol (signifying *mar*ine *pol*lution), whose aim is to stop dumping from oceangoing vessels. MARPOL (the official title is the Protocol of the International Convention for the Prevention of Pollution from Ships) has five sections, or annexes, each of which addresses particular types of ship-generated pollution (oil, hazardous liquids, etc.).

MARPOL Annex V, which focuses on ship-generated garbage, flatly forbids the dumping of plastics anywhere at sea. It also specifies how far from shore ships must be in order to dump other garbage such as glass, food, and paper.

Because the United States has ratified MARPOL, U.S. ships traveling anywhere in the world, as well as ships of any nationality traveling in U.S. waters (within two hundred miles of U.S. shores), are supposed to comply with MARPOL regulations. With the exception of some navy ships, MARPOL applies to vessels of all shapes and sizes, from rowboats on up.

MARPOL also states that certain ecologically sensitive regions may be classified as "Special Areas," where nothing other than finely ground food may be dumped. The Wider Caribbean Basin, which includes the Gulf of Mexico, has been designated one of these "Special Areas."

Unfortunately, ratifying MARPOL and its provisions is one thing, and enforcing them on the high seas is another. With oceans spanning more than 70 percent of the earth's surface, there is plenty of opportunity for old fishing gear, galley waste, packaging materials—virtually anything—to be inconspicuously heaved over the side of a ship. To complicate matters, many countries have not even ratified MARPOL.

Plastics continue to plague the oceans, and international marine debris experts are not yet convinced that MARPOL has had any appreciable effect on the situation. If ocean conditions are to improve, additional solutions must be found.

THE INTERNATIONAL COASTAL CLEANUP

On the third Saturday of September 1994, 4,743 volunteers in California began scouring the state's beaches and waterways in search of debris. In Ohio, scuba divers descended into the chill waters of Lake Erie to remove hundreds of beer cans, tennis shoes, and sundry other items from the lake bottom. In North Carolina, volunteers hoisted 319 tires from the New River. And at a single cleanup site in Puerto Rico, volunteers gathered enough debris to fill three hundred garbage bags—not including the more than 18,880 beer bottles they picked up. The event in which all of these people participated was the U.S. National Coastal Cleanup, itself part of an international coastal and waterway cleanup orchestrated by the Center for Marine Conservation. The annual event is impressive not only in its scope and size—participants in the 1994 U.S. National Cleanup numbered close to 140,000—but also in its intensity, for the three-hour hunt for trash spawns a year-round effort by the CMC to track down the sources of marine debris and work toward changing the habits of die-hard polluters. "One of the most critical things for people to realize," says Seba Sheavly, CMC International Coastal Cleanup coordinator, "is that the cleanup is far more than an aesthetic activity."

How It All Works

Volunteers usually arrive at the beach clad in shorts, sneakers, and sun hats. After splitting into pairs and receiving directions, trash bags, and data cards, they don gloves and begin picking up debris—quite literally, everything from cigarette butts to couches—along a designated stretch of beach or shoreline. And on their data sheets, they record every single item they find.

No volunteer who spends a morning at a cleanup, organizers say, ever looks at litter the same way again. After digging a couple hundred half-buried cigarette butts out of the sand, in other words, a volunteer is less likely to flick his own from the car window, or to remain silent when he sees someone else about to do so. Certainly, that person is more likely to pick up after a beach picnic with extra care. Following a cleanup, volunteers may begin searching the grocery shelves for less ornate packaging, or decide to use their own coffee mug each morning rather than buy a Styrofoam cup. A group of cleanup volunteers may decide to initiate a local recycling program, or even raise the issue of storm-drain debris at a town meeting. Quite simply, the event raises awareness. And, thanks to the media's interest in Coastal Cleanups, even those who have never considered joining an environmental effort are likely to hear about the event and learn something about debris through the evening news or the local newspaper.

Tracking Down the Polluters

From the data cards of tens of thousands of volunteers emerges what the Center for Marine Conservation refers to as a "moving snapshot," a brief glimpse of the condition of beaches, shorelines, and waterways throughout the country. Analyzing the evidence they have assembled, CMC researchers are able to deduce a great deal about where the debris is coming from and to try, through education and enforcement, to attack the problem at its myriad sources.

A certain number of items are fairly easy to trace: Tiny shampoo bottles turn up with the names of cruise lines embossed on them, and balloons can always be found advertising restaurants, shopping centers, real estate companies, and the like. For these types of items, the CMC writes to the parent company, pointing out the dangers debris can pose to the marine environment and soliciting their support in combating the problem (see "The Great Balloon Debate," page 30).

But in the vast majority of cases, tracking down the source of the debris is not nearly this simple. In most instances, therefore, marine debris experts rely on so-called indicator items, objects tied to particular activities, to formulate an idea of who is littering what. Certain items, for example, are associated with commercial fishing vessels. During the 1994 Cleanup, volunteers gleaned from the nation's shores nearly 86,000 pieces of plastic rope, more than 8,000 pieces of plastic netting, more than 6,700 plastic salt bags (for treating catches), close to 14,500 rubber gloves (for sorting catches), and more than 14,000 plastic buoys—all suggesting that illegal dumping from commercial fishing vessels remained rampant.

Other studies have gone farther in identifying the culprits responsible for coastal garbage. The National Park Service, for example, carried out a rigorous investigation of marine debris on Padre Island National Seashore; Padre Island is an island off the Texas coast whose shores are considered some of the most heavily polluted in the United States. By examining more than forty thousand items that washed ashore over the course of a year, investigators were able to show that 13 percent of the debris was linked to oil and gas platforms, and that a full 30 percent stemmed from shrimping vessels. An additional 35 percent, they suspect, is also associated with the shrimping industry. Incidentally, many of the shrimping-related debris items were found riddled with distinctive, diamond-shaped holes, indicating that they had been mistaken for food by sea turtles.

Cigarette Butts: Still the Leader of the Pack
Year after year at the International Coastal Cleanup, cigarette butts have earned the dubious distinction of being the most plentiful item collected. During the 1994 Cleanup, for example, some 1.3 million (the equivalent of sixty-four thousand packs of cigarettes) were picked up, many the by-product of long, lazy days at the beach. Contrary to what many people believe, cigarette butts are not biodegradable: The filters are made from a form of plastic called cellulose acetate. And cigarette butts are more than merely unsightly: They have been found in the stomachs of seabirds, turtles, and other marine animals.

The Perennial Problem of Plastics
Since the first U.S. National Coastal Cleanup, plastics have hovered at around 60 percent of all debris found. (Cigarette butts are not included in this figure.) Sadly, wildlife seems to bear the brunt of this problem: During the 1994 Cleanup,

volunteers came across eighty-two entangled animals, the overwhelming majority of them entrapped in monofilament line, plastic netting, plastic strapping bands, plastic bags, roping, or six-pack rings. Among the victims were cormorants, blue herons, doves, pelicans, seagulls, an eel, a mynah bird, sea urchins, even a mouse trapped in a plastic bag. Out of all these animals, volunteers were able to release only a single seagull.

Thanks to the publicity the Cleanup has generated, however, some positive changes are being seen on the plastics front. The Society of the Plastics Industry, for example, has come on board as an important sponsor of the Cleanup and has initiated several campaigns to educate those industries that contribute more than their share of marine debris. Certain plastics manufacturers, as well, have taken the initiative to make their own products safer, and to keep them out of the marine environment. ITW Hi-Cone, for example, the country's largest manufacturer of six-pack rings, has developed six-pack rings that are photodegradable (that is, that break into tiny pieces when exposed to sunlight). But because a photodegradable ring can require as long as thirty-five days to degrade—plenty of time for an animal to become ensnared in a ring and die—Hi-Cone has gone a step farther by designing a product whose rings can be broken with the single pull of a tab. And to convey the message that even the safest product should not be discarded in the marine environment, the company has even started a recycling program for its products (see "Waging a War with Big Sweep," page 24).

Beyond the Statistics: Some Items of Interest
During every Coastal Cleanup, volunteers rid local coastlines

and waterways of staggering quantities of what might be considered "typical" debris. During the 1994 Cleanup, close to 35,000 fast-food containers, roughly 122,000 Styrofoam cups, and more than 386,000 plastic bags were bagged and carried off in the space of a few hours. But the Cleanup is also something of a treasure hunt, for one never knows what might be hidden in a clump of seaweed or barely submerged beneath the water's surface. Like all Cleanups before it, the 1994 event yielded some unusual items. Nationwide, volunteers carted off nine refrigerators, thirteen televisions, six couches, twelve mattresses, eleven sets of box springs, a beanbag chair, an electric blender, and even a couple of kitchen sinks. They cleaned the shores of everything from pacifiers to hula hoops to an inflatable plastic woman. They hauled away a submerged Pontiac Fiero and fifty-four thousand pieces of clothing. And they stuffed their garbage bags with rat traps and a hamster wheel; marijuana, cocaine, and hashish; fake fingernails; even a bag of undelivered mail. California waterways yielded their own treasures, including a wedding dress, a full bottle of Prozac, a 9mm handgun, and a VW bus.

At the Heart of the Battle

Were there not such a hearty turnout each year for the International Coastal Cleanup and cleanups like it, those whose business it is to study and combat marine debris would have no raw material from which to work. Volunteers are essential to the battle against debris. Seba Sheavly, of the Center for Marine Conservation, is emphatic about this point. "Unlike oil spills or global warming," she writes, "marine debris is one pollution problem that individuals can change by direct, individual action. The purpose of collecting trash is to bring it all home: the sources, the problems, and ultimately, the solutions."

FOSTERING COASTAL STEWARDSHIP THROUGH ADOPT-A-BEACH

Adopt-A-Beach is just what the name says: a program for those who want to make a commitment to caring for a beach, usually by cleaning it up throughout the year. The Adopt-A-Beach program varies from state to state, with California's program, run by the California Coastal Commission, offering a glimpse at the tremendous potential behind the "Adopt" concept.

In California, groups that adopt a section of beach or coastline generally promise to carry out cleanups at least three times each year (with one cleanup coinciding with the International Coastal Cleanup in September). As one might expect, beach adoption is popular with Scout troops, seniors organizations, environmental clubs, civic and church groups, and the like. But the program attracts less conventional groups as well, such as the South Bay Nudists, who routinely carry out their cleanups without benefit of clothing. In all, roughly two hundred organizations, representing some ten thousand volunteers, currently care for California beaches on an ongoing basis.

Adopt-A-Beach gets a big boost from corporations and nonprofit organizations, which donate funding, volunteers, and in-kind services to help make the program successful. Twice a year, for example, hundreds of employees from Southern California Edison's coastal generating plants turn out to scour the shores for debris. Members of the Surfrider Foundation, a coastal conservation group with chapters along the California coast, direct cleanups throughout the year. Even the Adopt-A-Beach publicity campaign, which reaches out to its audience through public service announcements, informational brochures, and TV and radio talk-show appearances, is funded through the generosity of a prominent national advertising agency.

One of the program's strongest suits is its work with students, who are introduced to coastal issues in the classroom through an exciting, innovative curriculum, developed in partnership with the Center for Marine Conservation, called "Save Our Seas." In this curriculum, students from kindergarten on up learn not just about debris, but about the maze of issues surrounding it—everything from why ships have such difficulties in stowing their own garbage, to how marine animals are impacted by debris, to the ways that "reduce, reuse, and recycle" can be applied to the students' daily lives. The payoff for all the classroom work comes in the form of a field trip to the coast, where students carry out cleanups under the supervision of an Adopt-A-Beach beach manager. And it is here, on the beach, that much of what they have learned in the classroom hits home. As Jack Liebster, director of public affairs for the California Coastal Commission, points out, "Few children are not moved by the plight of entangled animals, or the wonder of a tide pool, or the graceful, soaring line of a flight of pelicans. The coast becomes their classroom, a wonderful natural laboratory, exciting and intruiging."

Evidence suggests that students find the program fun and inspiring. In Los Angeles, for example, students from Venice

High School followed up their beach cleanup by challenging students from another school to a recycling contest. They then set about gathering aluminum cans, and in short order filled their classroom with some thirty-seven thousand of them. Redeeming the cans, they earned enough money to purchase acreage in a Costa Rican rain forest so that the land could be set aside for conservation.

The mission of California's Adopt-A-Beach program extends far beyond the aesthetics of a sandy stretch. Like the International Coastal Cleanup, Adopt-A-Beach uses cleanups as a vehicle to promote greater understanding of coastal issues and to foster a sense of stewardship toward the marine environment. "In its most fundamental essence," writes Liebster, "Adopt-A-Beach is about people taking personal responsibility for the coast and the environment. By participating they make an eloquent statement that each of us is obligated to care for the coast as if it were our own front yard."

A LOT TO BE LEARNED FROM TEXAS

Texas, a state where coastal cleanups have taken root and flourished, is in some ways a coastal conservation success story. In other ways, Texas illustrates the frustrating, complex, and somewhat intractable nature of marine debris.

The First Texas Coastal Cleanup

In January 1986, Linda Maraniss took her first walk on a Texas beach and was shocked at what she saw. Maraniss, who had just left the Washington, D.C., headquarters of the Center for Marine Conservation to open a regional office in

Austin, had read plenty about the subject of marine debris. Nevertheless, the profusion of glass bottles, egg cartons, and plastic milk jugs that covered the sand served as a rude surprise. "It looked like a landfill," she recalls. "Everything that had ever been written about plastics in the coastal environment could be seen on Texas beaches that day."

As long as she remained in Texas, Maraniss decided, fighting for a cleaner coast would have to be her top priority. A well-organized cleanup, she believed, would not only improve the quality of the shoreline, but would draw people's attention to the severity of the debris situation. Maraniss was also anxious for the United States to ratify the international treaty known as MARPOL Annex V, which forbids the dumping of plastics at sea. "I knew that other countries had ratified Annex V," she says, "and I thought that if people were more informed about debris and about plastics in particular, they might put some pressure on Congress to ratify it as well."

Working closely with her colleagues in Washington, Maraniss set about organizing the first Texas Coastal Cleanup. An official logo was developed, "Be a Beach Buddy" was coined as a slogan, and a data card was created so that volunteers could record every single piece of debris they came across. In May, funding for the cleanup was secured.

At that point, Maraniss realized that most of the work ahead would have to be carried out solo. Guided by a state map, she began traveling the Texas coast all the way from Mexico to Louisiana, locating likely cleanup sites, recruiting volunteers to serve as cleanup coordinators, ironing out logistical difficulties, and talking with local media about the upcoming event. Bringing together representatives of the U.S.

Navy; the merchant shipping, petroleum, and plastics industries; government officials; and others, she formed a Marine Debris Steering Committee to help shed light on the debris problem.

The first Texas Coastal Cleanup took place on the third Saturday in September. It was a remarkable effort, with three thousand volunteers turning out to clean roughly 122 miles of coastline. One hundred twenty-four tons of debris were collected. With information gleaned from volunteers' data cards, Maraniss and her committee formulated twenty-nine suggestions for reducing marine debris on a national and local level. One of these suggestions resulted in the formation of the Texas Adopt-A-Beach program.

The committee also used the data to create a formal, detailed report that was submitted to Congress. In December 1988, MARPOL Annex V was implemented in the United States.

Each year since its inception, the Cleanup has expanded. By 1988 it had become national in scope, and by the following year, it had extended beyond U.S. borders.

Texas Adopt-A-Beach

Through Adopt-A-Beach, Texas continues to be a leader in the fight for cleaner beaches. The Texas Coastal Cleanup that takes place each September, for example, is now complemented by a spring event called the "Great Texas Beach Trash-Off." In addition, the entire stretch of Texas coast has been adopted by groups pledging to carry out at least one additional cleanup each year. Even state prisoners get in on the act: Every few months, well-supervised groups of inmates forgo other privileges for the chance to travel to the beach and pick up litter. Adopt-A-Beach also sponsors activities to raise awareness in the general public: In years past children have taken part in the "Get a Line on Litter" poster contest, while adults have created sculptures from marine debris and entered them in the "Trash for Art's Sake" competition.

The good news, says Roxanne Rouse, Texas Adopt-A-Beach coordinator, is that Texans are becoming increasingly aware of the debris issue. Recycling programs are growing, litter on some beaches is picked up as quickly as it is dropped, and—in some cities, at least—anyone who casually throws a cigarette butt onto the ground can expect to be challenged by passersby. The bad news is that all of the awareness in the world will not come close to eradicating the problem. Because of the way the currents swirl through the Gulf of Mexico—often referred to as the toilet bowl effect—oceanborne debris originating anywhere in the Gulf, whether from oil platforms, shrimp and fishing boats, cruise ships, or international freighters, is picked up and carried right onto the beaches of Texas or Mexico.

Rouse likes to illustrate the extent of the problem by recalling the 1994 Texas Coastal Cleanup, which took place only four months after the Great Texas Beach Trash-Off. During the cleanup, volunteers covered 190 miles of coastline and gathered 462,000 pounds of trash. In Florida, by contrast, volunteers covering nearly a thousand *more* miles of coast picked up one hundred thousand fewer pounds of debris.

Although Rouse envisions no easy cure for the problem, she is encouraged by the attitudes of Texans. "I see a real hunger for information. People want to know how they can help out, or whom to contact to lodge a complaint. They get angry when they see their beaches covered in garbage, or when they see a dead turtle washed up on shore, a plastic bag sticking out of its mouth."

Translating this kind of concern into cleaner beaches, however, remains a tremendous challenge.

WAGING A WAR WITH BIG SWEEP

In North Carolina, the annual Coastal Cleanup has taken on a life of its own. "Big Sweep" (the name not only of the cleanup but also of the dynamic organization that runs it) targets debris before it ever gets tossed in the sand, thrown over the side of a boat, or washed down a river toward the coast.

While it is no secret that inland waterways contribute significantly to the coastal debris problem, Big Sweep organizers were the first in the U.S. National Coastal Cleanup to take their cleanup efforts statewide. Today, Big Sweep volunteers not only walk the state's beaches, but they also paddle, motor, and wade through lakes, rivers, and even ponds and streams in search of debris.

Through a hard-hitting, well-focused educational campaign, Big Sweep has also taken aim at those who might be categorized as repeat environmental offenders. When Big Sweep organizers took a look at data from several consecutive cleanups, they realized that nearly half of what was being picked up consisted of fast-food containers, cigarette butts, bait cups, fishing line, pop cans and bottles—all of which pointed the finger at recreational fishermen, boaters, and beachgoers.

To reach boaters, Big Sweep manufactured thousands of reusable, mesh litter bags, and distributed them to boating safety classes, fishing tournaments, and similar sorts of events. And even if a boater missed the opportunity to get a litter bag, it would have been difficult to miss the posters hung in marinas, bait and tackle shops, and parks during the summer of 1992, featuring popular NASCAR driver Richard Petty and the message: "Don't Splash Your Trash." Petty also donated his time to record a series of public service announcements conveying the same message.

Because cigarette butts consistently turned up as the most prevalent type of debris, Big Sweep decided to home in on smokers. North Carolina tobacco company R.J. Reynolds joined the effort, first by serving as a cleanup sponsor, then by putting together a catchy public awareness campaign featuring the motto: "Don't Leave Your Butt on the Beach." To make it easier for smokers to do the right thing, the company also manufactured handy foil-lined pocket ashtrays, thousands of which have been handed out to Tar Heel smokers. And smokers, it appears, have responded: Since 1992, Big Sweep volunteers have recorded a slow but steady decline in the number of butts they are finding along waterways.

Big Sweep has even approached the boaters, fishermen, and beachgoers of tomorrow through two classroom programs that introduce students to marine debris and related issues. Both "Ripples," a program for nine-to-eleven-year-olds, and "Splish Splash," for five-to-seven-year-olds, have been well received. In schools where the programs have been used, students have written letters to state legislators about water pollution, lobbied against school balloon releases, and embarked on six-pack-ring recycling projects.

Throughout North Carolina, dozens of corporations, state agencies, television stations, power companies, boating associations, and environmental groups have helped champion the cause of clean beaches and waterways. First Citizens Bank, for example, title sponsor of the event, provides extensive financial assistance, staff support, management advice, and in-kind services. And at every Big Sweep, First Citizens Bank employees can be counted on to make up about one-tenth of the volunteer force.

There is little doubt that North Carolina's beaches and waterways are measurably cleaner—and staying that way—thanks to Big Sweep. In fact, thirty-five fewer tons of debris were picked up during the 1994 cleanup than during the previous year's event. The Big Sweep theme—"You are the solution to water pollution"—is being heard not only by those who pick up litter once a year, but also by those who in former days created much of the problem.

UNDERWATER DEBRIS: AN INVISIBLE MENACE

Waters as smooth as glass can hide a messy, dangerous array of debris beneath the surface: plastic sheeting that smothers underwater plant life, steel fishing leader that cuts through delicate sponges, and monofilament line that becomes tangled up in corals. This is the world that divers see, and the motivation for a small but expanding number of volunteers who dive with the express purpose of removing underwater debris.

The most prevalent type of underwater debris, says Bruce Ryan, coordinator for the underwater portion of the National

Coastal Cleanup, is monofilament line. "Seeing what mono-filament line can do underwater," he says, "will boggle your mind." Bait-sized fish are the first to become entangled. When the tiny fish die, their decomposing bodies attract crabs. They, in turn, become entangled, die, and attract larger fish. "The line becomes a perpetual killing machine," says Ryan, "and the whole process is a complete and utter waste." Judging from the reports of divers, heavily fished waters are full of discarded line and fishing debris. In 1995, during a two-hour dive near Florida's Ft. Pickens Jetty and Pier, thir-teen divers gathered 8,448 feet of monofilament line, 10 nets, 892 lead weights, and 356 fishing hooks, and came across 6 dead, entangled animals. Fortunately, they were able to dis-entangle more than a hundred live animals—everything from sea horses on up.

Divers do not have to wait for the annual Coastal Cleanup to carry out a dive in search of debris. Ryan suggests choos-ing an area where monofilament line is likely to be abundant, such as near a bridge, jetty, or pier, and learning the "dos and don'ts" of underwater cleanups before proceeding. Removing debris from a reef can be a delicate task, and a well-inten-tioned but poorly trained diver, one who might decide to yank monofilament line off a coral rather than carefully snip-ping it, could do far more harm than good. Fishermen, says Ryan, are very appreciative of divers' efforts to clean a site, and are usually more than willing to stop fishing for a few hours while the divers work.

Divers will be heartened to learn that Berkley, a fishing-line manufacturer based in Idaho, runs a recycling program for used monofilament line. Since 1990, the company has collected and recycled the equivalent of more than five million miles of old fishing line.

CRUISE SHIP CONTROVERSY

It is perhaps a double insult that cruise ships, whose livelihoods are linked to the allure of peaceful, pristine waters, have for years been such despoilers of the world's oceans. But thanks to a public outcry, practices on board some of the world's luxury liners are starting to change.

Evidence of widespread dumping from cruise liners has come from two sources. Through the International Coastal Cleanup, the Center for Marine Conservation keeps tabs on how much of the debris picked up each year is directly traceable to cruise ships. (Items such as tiny shampoo bottles, swizzle sticks, and shoeshine kits are likely to have come from cruise ships; many lines make identification far easier by embossing these objects with their names or logos.) As late as 1991, fourteen cruise lines were represented by their debris at the international cleanup event.

Complementing the evidence that washes up on shore are eyewitness accounts of dumping. Passengers have reported seeing plenty of clandestine waste-disposal practices, especially during the wee hours of the morning. And brimming garbage bags are just the beginning: Observers have watched as toxic chemicals, mattresses, deck furniture, and even the contents of a recycling container have been heaved overboard.

Since the early 1990s, however, things have started to change, thanks in part to the increasingly activist role taken by cruise ship passengers. Armed with "cruise ship information packets" from the Center for Marine Conservation, many passengers have learned what can be legally dumped from a ship and what cannot, and know precisely how to document any suspicious dumping incident.

In 1991, two astute passengers aboard a Princess liner observed crew members as they threw twenty plastic bags overboard near the Florida Keys. They videotaped the incident and passed their information on to the U.S. Coast Guard; and two years later, in the first criminal penalty ever to be imposed on a cruise line, Princess Cruises was fined $500,000. (Incidentally, when *I Witness Video* aired a story about the episode, complete with videotape footage, the show received nineteen phone calls from viewers wanting to report similar incidents.) For many in the cruise industry, the conviction represented a turning point.

Princess Cruises, to its credit, decided not to sweep the incident under the rug, but to completely revamp its waste-disposal practices. The cruise line's current, radically improved system for handling garbage includes recycling, source reduction, and some creative methods for holding crew members accountable for their part in the waste-disposal process. Under this system, plastics, cardboard, paper, glass, tin, and food are all separated on board, to be either incinerated, offloaded on shore, or recycled. (Food, when finely ground, can go straight into the ocean.) At every level, practices have changed. Disposable plastic drinking glasses, for example, once used on deck in areas where glass is forbidden, have been replaced by plastic tumblers heavy enough to be sent through a dishwasher. Plastic bottles for cosmetic amenities such as shampoo and conditioner have been replaced by wax-impregnated cardboard containers that can be incinerated on board, a change that results in the company's using and discarding some seven and a half million fewer plastic containers each year.

Unfortunately, certain cruise lines have responded less commendably to the debris issue, and have simply removed their name or logo from items that may find their way to shore. But many of the companies seem to be rethinking their waste-disposal practices, and hoping, in the process, to benefit from a new, environmentally friendly image. One indication of this change of heart can be seen in the annual Coastal Cleanup: During the 1994 Cleanup, the debris of only one cruise line could be found.

A DELIGHT OR A DANGER: THE GREAT BALLOON DEBATE

No discussion of marine debris would be complete without a look at balloons. Releasing balloons into the atmosphere may seem to be a beautiful and dramatic way to celebrate a festive or momentous occasion. But as peaceful as the balloons appear as they float into the atmosphere, the thought of what happens after they disappear from sight is anything but comforting. Balloon releases, in which hundreds, thousands, even hundreds of thousands of balloons are simultaneously set free, are the subject of a long-standing controversy concerning marine debris and the welfare of marine animals.

For anyone who has walked the beach and taken a close look at the debris underfoot, chances are balloons have not been at the top of the list. And yet, during the 1994 International Coastal Cleanup, volunteers picked up more than thirty-six thousand balloons or balloon fragments. They also came across a dead loon and gull entangled in balloons and their ribbons.

Plenty of balloons, whole and in fragments, have been found in the stomachs of seabirds, sea turtles, and marine mammals. In 1987 an emaciated, thirteen-hundred-pound leatherback turtle, its top shell marred by a three-foot gash, washed up dead on the New Jersey shore. Snaking through the animal's intestines was a three-foot blue ribbon, attached to a balloon whose knot was blocking the opening between the intestines and the stomach. Those who examined the turtle speculated that once the balloon lodged in its digestive tract, the turtle grew weak from starvation. Unable to dive, the animal was probably killed by a speedboat.

In response to growing concern over the role of balloons in the environment, the Balloon Council has mounted a campaign purporting to set the record straight. According to the Council, voluntary safety guidelines specify that only latex (that is, rubber) balloons, hand-tied and not attached to ribbons, should be used in mass releases. These balloons decompose, according to the Council, at about the same rate an oak leaf might. (Mylar balloons, which are plastic and not biodegradable, are simply too expensive to use in mass releases.) Furthermore, when balloons are released en masse, the vast majority of them rise about five miles, then fracture into tiny pieces that fall back to earth. If these pieces litter the shore, they do so in negligible amounts. And if an animal happens to eat a piece of balloon, the argument continues, the latex is likely to pass harmlessly through the animal's digestive system. According to the Council, a balloon has never been indicted as the sole cause of an animal's death.

Many of the Balloon Council's arguments have been disputed. Nonetheless, the decision as to whether or not to release balloons, either singly or en masse, ultimately lands in the lap of the balloon consumer. How much debris should be considered "insignificant"? Does a balloon destined to decompose in weeks, months, or years constitute a threat to marine wildlife as long as it remains intact? Is the simultaneous release of thousands of balloons merely a feast for the eyes, or a socially acceptable form of litter?

Six states (California, Connecticut, Florida, New York, Tennessee, and Virginia) have made their decisions, and have passed laws that restrict or prohibit mass balloon releases. Other states are considering similar legislation.

Fortunately, there are plenty of wonderful alternatives to balloon releases. Arches, columns, and canopies constructed from balloons, as well as balloon sculpture contests, are both beautiful and environmentally friendly. Norwegian Cruise Lines, since learning of the dangers balloons can pose to the environment, has started decorating its ships with thousands of balloons that stay firmly anchored in place. Another way to celebrate is by staging "balloon drops," in which hundreds or even thousands of balloons, suspended near the ceiling, are released en masse over the heads of partygoers.

The Center for Marine Conservation considers balloons to be potentially deadly debris. There is virtually no difference, the center points out, between releasing 250,000 balloons and dropping 250,000 plastic bags over the side of a ship. The Balloon Council takes a different stance. "Don't let environmental 'Grinches,'" it warns, "spoil your party."

OTHER WAYS TO RAISE AWARENESS

Storm-Drain Stenciling

DUMPING POLLUTES

KEEP POLLUTANTS OUT: DRAINS TO LAKE

DUMP NO WASTE: DRAINS TO BAY

Messages like these, stenciled in brightly colored, bold letters on storm drains throughout the country, remind passersby that what starts out on the pavement will inevitably wind up in the water. Toss a plastic lid into the gutter, and before long it can be found floating along the surface of a bay or littering the sands of a beach.

From towns such as Alliance, Ohio, to Los Angeles, California, small, informal groups of volunteers are putting their stamp on storm drains to point out the inherent connection between people's actions and the quality of their local waters. Many of these groups belong to a national stenciling network run by the Center for Marine Conservation called "Million Points of Blight"—the name referring to the million or more storm drains the CMC hopes to have stenciled by the year 2000.

In the Los Angeles area, volunteers from a program called "Gutter Patrol" take to the streets once a month, stenciling storm drains and distributing brilliantly colored bilingual door hangers. At a glance, the hangers describe urban runoff and explain how each person can contribute to a cleaner Santa Monica Bay. Gutter Patrol is run by an organization called Heal the Bay, which is dedicated to improving the quality of the bay's waters.

Candy Ibarra, Gutter Patrol coordinator, finds that in many of the neighborhoods where the program is in effect, residents are shocked to learn that what goes into a storm drain arrives in coastal waters completely untreated. And within a given community, the program's most immediate and dramatic impact is always on the children. "If you present the message in the right way," says Ibarra, "children will learn it, get excited by it, and go back and tell their parents. And kids," she adds, "can be pretty persistent."

Volunteers, on the other hand, relish the fact that the program covers a lot of ground in a short period of time. During a few hours' work, five or six volunteers can stencil dozens of storm drains and distribute hundreds of door hangers. Stenciling, moreover, seems to kill two birds with one stone. "It's a great way of dealing with a neighborhood's debris problem," says Ibarra, "and cleaning up the ocean at the same time."

Educating the Boating Community

There are plenty of community-based programs designed to help raise awareness about marine debris in the minds of boaters and fishermen. What could be simpler than a program, aptly named "Pier Pressure," in which volunteers spend a day at a local marina, handing out literature and garbage bags and discussing debris issues with boaters? Another program, called "Stow It, Don't Throw It," takes place at fishing tournaments, where competitors are given a short talk about the dangers of marine debris and provided with empty garbage bags as they depart the dock each morning. Upon returning at the end of the day with a stuffed garbage bag, each competitor receives a raffle ticket for a prize to be given away at the end of the tournament.

These small-scale educational programs have the advantage of being low budget, easy to plan, and extremely flexible. And virtually any group—from Cub Scouts on up—can carry them out effectively. If a program is planned well in advance and is undertaken by an enthusiastic and dedicated cadre of volunteers, it may be interesting enough to attract the attention of the media, which helps spread the word about marine debris to an even larger audience.

For those interested in tackling a more challenging endeavor, there is certainly ample opportunity. In 1987, Fran Recht of Newport, Oregon, initiated a program to encourage commercial and recreational fishermen to bring their trash back to shore. Working in partnership with the local port and the National Marine Fisheries Service, Recht devoted much of her time to educating fishermen about the dangers of marine debris, and went to great lengths so that it would be easy and convenient for them to off-load their refuse at port. The fishermen responded by returning vast quantities of debris to shore, and by separating cardboard, wood, metal, cable, and even netting so that they could be recycled. The program, in short, has been tremendously successful. Because a program such as this entails research and planning, as well as the close cooperation of marina operators, fishermen, and local waste-collection agencies, Recht warns against undertaking such an endeavor without considerable forethought.

COASTWEEKS: A CELEBRATION OF THE COAST

"Celebrate! Educate! Participate!" is the rallying cry of Coastweeks, an annual celebration of the nation's coasts and waterways. From Cape Cod to California, Coastweeks provides participants with a wealth of opportunities to enjoy their coastal environment, offering everything from wetland walks and salt-marsh cruises to bird-watches and fish-hatchery tours, lectures, conferences and workshops, seafood festivals and whale-watching expeditions, even an overnight at a historic Massachusetts lighthouse. The hope is that while joining in the festivities, people will renew their appreciation of their shores, develop a better understanding of coastal issues, and ultimately help to protect and preserve their own coasts and waterways. "It's a celebration, a festival," says Coastweeks founder Barbara Fegan, "and by participating, people can't help but learn."

One Woman's Inspiration

Fegan, who lives in the small town of Wellfleet, on Cape Cod, says the idea for a coastal celebration was in fact one born out of frustration. In 1982, as coastal issues specialist for the League of Women Voters, Fegan felt that the general public was not nearly involved enough in coastal issues, and that without public participation, coastal policy could not move forward. There had to be some way, she reasoned, to bring people into the discourse, to pique their interest and educate them about coastal issues at the same time.

It was during what Fegan refers to as a "two in the morning *aha!*" that the idea came to her: a week, loosely organized around the coastal theme, in which people could partake in any number of coast-related activities. "You have to get the people interested," says Fegan. "You have to give them information, let them know what their stake is, and tell them what to do next. And you have to make it fun."

Then, as now, Coastweeks represented a remarkable partnership between public agencies and private organizations. The concept of a national Coastweek was first endorsed by the governor of Massachusetts and the League of Women Voters, then by the Coast Alliance, the Coastal States Organization, the Coastal Society, and the Sierra Club. Fegan, however, wanted to see whether the idea would appeal to a larger audience. Using her first Social Security check to buy stamps and a new typewriter ribbon, she sent out a four-page invitation to coastal advocates among the general public, explaining the concept of Coastweek, suggesting a handful of activities, and asking whether the respondents might care to sponsor something along these lines in their own communities. The response, says Fegan, "was utterly gratifying."

When the first coastal celebration took place in 1983, writes Fegan, more than a thousand activities were offered, "ranging from beach parties to major conferences, from canoe trips to nature walks." Coastweek soon expanded to become Coastweeks, eventually linked up with the International Coastal Cleanup, which now serves as the international program's kick-off event. And besides catching on from an entertainment perspective, Coastweeks has proved to have educational merit, for in 1990 Congress reauthorized the Coastal Zone Management Act, something that might never have taken place without the support of an informed public.

Moving Beyond the Coast

Each state celebrates Coastweeks differently. Washington, for example, has shaped and molded the event into a month-long environmental extravaganza. In fact, Washington Coastweeks is no longer Coastweeks at all: It is now Washington Waterweeks, a statewide festival focusing on shorelines, rivers, lakes, streams, and even "your neighborhood watershed." Through all manner of offerings, Waterweeks encourages participants to make the link between their day-to-day activities and the health of their local waterways.

In 1994 Washington Waterweeks offered some 220 activities, including wetland walks and a mudflat safari; canoe and kayak trips and water-treatment plant tours; storm-drain stenciling projects and beach cleanups; workshops on subjects from aquatic plants to lake advocacy; hazardous waste roundups; half a dozen activities related to salmon and their habitat; an Oysterfest for the hungry; poetry readings, museum tours, and a play for the more cerebral; and for kids, activities such as Watershed Willy puppet shows, a Fish Fun Fest, a Paddlin' Pond Pals Preschool/ Parent Hike, and Tadpoles with Tales and Fish-a-licious storytimes.

"We provide a whole range of approaches that are fun and that encourage people to 'get their feet wet' in learning about their beaches, wetlands, and watersheds," says Tim Gates, Waterweeks coordinator. "What Waterweeks offers is an invitation to get closer to your environment."

Fegan, who in 1994 happily passed Coastweeks on to the Center for Marine Conservation, believes the concept of a coastal celebration has lasted because people are inherently fascinated by land, by water, and by the regions where the two come together. "Coastweeks is simply a period of time," she says, "when the nation looks at its coasts, analyzes them, and appreciates them."

FOR MORE INFORMATION

To receive a marine debris information packet, a cruise line information packet, or general information about Coastweeks, contact the Center for Marine Conservation at its headquarters in Washington, D.C.:

CENTER FOR MARINE CONSERVATION
1725 DeSales Street, NW
Washington, D.C. 20036
(202) 429-5609

For information on the International Coastal Cleanup, general beach cleanup activities, or the Million Points of Blight storm-drain stenciling network, contact the Center for Marine Conservation at its Atlantic Regional Office:

CENTER FOR MARINE CONSERVATION
Atlantic Regional Office
306A Buckroe Avenue
Hampton, VA 23664
(804) 851-6734

For information about underwater cleanups, contact:

CENTER FOR MARINE CONSERVATION
Florida Regional Office
Bayfront Tower
One Beach Drive SE, Suite 304
St. Petersburg, FL 33701
(813) 895-2188

MARPOL placards and citizen report forms may be obtained from the U.S. Coast Guard:

COMMANDANT (G-MRO)
The U.S. Coast Guard
2100 Second Street, SW
Washington, D.C. 20593

To recycle monofilament fishing line, you may send the line directly to:

BERKLEY
Recycling Center
P.O. Box 456
Spirit Lake, ID 51360-0456

For information about Gutter Patrol or other programs involved in cleaning up Santa Monica Bay, contact:

HEAL THE BAY
2701 Ocean Park Boulevard
Suite 150
Santa Monica, CA 90405
(310) 581-4188

Campaigning for Cleaner Waters

I n battling debris, one at least has the advantage of a visible foe. Polluted waters are not always so easy to discern. Beachgoers may begin complaining of sore throats, infected eyes, or stomach ailments. Fish living near outfall pipes may become plagued with liver tumors or fin rot. A coral reef may begin wasting away. There is no single indicator for impaired waters.

There seems to be a common misconception, moreover, about how our waters become polluted. For many people, the term "water pollution" conjures up an image of a brown froth spewing from a pipe outside an industrial facility, or of a steady stream of murky liquid flowing from a sewage-treatment plant. Filthy discharge of this type, however, termed point-source pollution because it can be traced to a particular point of origin, is no longer the threat to coastal waterways it was in decades past. Not only has point-source pollution been targeted by the 1972 Clean Water Act, but because its source is usually easy to identify, cleaning it up is a relatively straightforward endeavor. Today, a far greater threat to the nation's waterways is nonpoint-source pollution, which stems from diverse, unrelated, and often invisible sources.

Nonpoint-source pollution, commonly referred to as polluted runoff, is anything that is picked up by rainwater or snowmelt traveling to the nearest waterway. Residues from gasoline and motor oil that accumulate on roads and highways, fertilizers overzealously applied to lawns, gardens, and fields, uncontained cow manure from farmers' feedlots, plastic cups, cigarette butts, grass clippings, dog feces that are left along sidewalks—all of these become polluted runoff as they flow into streams or are washed into storm drains that empty into lakes, rivers, bays, and the open ocean.

The Environmental Protection Agency (E.P.A.) has identified polluted runoff as the single greatest threat to the health of our nation's waters. And yet, because so much of this pollution stems from the innumerable daily activities that make up modern life—pouring things down the gutter, for example, or spraying the garden—the prospect of stemming the problem solely through government regulation is an unlikely one: Imagine the difficulty involved in regulating the use of fertilizers, pesticides, or herbicides on homeowners' lawns and gardens.

A more useful strategy centers on education—showing people how seemingly innocuous substances can become hazards in an aquatic environment, and pointing out how each of us can resist contributing to the problem. Here, for a start, is a brief rundown of five prominent contaminants in polluted runoff.

Sediment

It may come as a surprise that sediment—gravel, sand, or plain old dirt—can devastate an underwater ecosystem. But each year, more than one billion tons of it wash into the nation's waterways, at a huge cost to aquatic plants and animals. Sediment clouds the water, depriving underwater vegetation of the light needed to carry out photosynthesis. And once the sediment settles, it blankets the bottom substrate, smothering fish spawning habitat, fish eggs, newly hatched fish, even the bugs that fish feed on. In the Northwest, thousands of miles of freshwater streams, whose oxygen-rich, pebbly bottoms serve as spawning grounds for salmon and trout, have been damaged or destroyed by sedimentation from logging, road building, agriculture, and urbanization.

Often, sediment carries toxins along with it as it washes into waterways. And unlike some other pollutants, it does not dissolve in water, but merely settles to the bottom. For this reason, it can become a repeat offender, wreaking havoc in a freshwater or estuarine environment every time the water gets stirred up (see "The Keeper Programs," page 61).

Nutrients

Although it seems unlikely that nitrogen and phosphorus, both vital to normal plant growth, could be damaging to the underwater ecosystem, these two nutrients can suck the life out of a healthy estuary through a process known as eutrophication. Upon entering the water, nitrogen and phosphorus stimulate bursts of alga growth, called "blooms," that block the light needed by bottom-dwelling vegetation. Eventually the algae dies. Bacteria then break down the dead algae, and in the process consume the water's stores of dissolved oxygen. Once the oxygen levels become intolerably low, adult fish are forced to find new habitat, while fish eggs and larvae, as well as shellfish, simply die off. Nutrient overenrichment (often referred to as "nutrient loading") has been identified as the most significant and pervasive type of pollution threatening the Chesapeake Bay.

Pathogens

Polluted runoff also takes the form of pathogens—disease-causing bacteria and viruses—that find their way into waterways from leaky sewer and septic systems, untreated boat bilge, and animal feces. When shellfish beds are closed, or beaches are suddenly declared unsafe for swimming, high pathogen counts are usually the reason. Among the illnesses associated with bacteria-contaminated waters are gastroenteritis, dysentery, and hepatitis.

Toxins

Toxins also travel freely into the nation's harbors, bays, and beach waters. Household cleaners, paints, and solvents that are disposed of in the laundry-room sink are filled with toxins; so are the motor oil and antifreeze that get poured down the garage drain. Because residential septic systems and municipal sewage-treatment plants are geared primarily toward the removal of organic matter, and not toxins, many of these dangerous substances move right through the system and eventually find their way into groundwater, streams, and estuaries. (Technically, this type of pollution is considered point source.) Other toxins, whether from car-exhaust particulates or gasoline, are washed off roads and into storm drains after every rain. Poisonous lawn and garden products continually leach into the groundwater that replenishes nearby streams and lakes. In all, an estimated 740 million pounds of toxic chemicals flow into the nation's waterways each year.

Many of these poisonous substances are not easily broken down. As a result, once toxins have been ingested by small aquatic organisms, they tend to move up the food chain, accumulating in greater and greater quantities until they reach dangerous concentrations in the bodies of predatory fish and birds.

Debris
Perhaps the most aesthetically offensive of all polluted runoff is debris (see chapter 1). Even biodegradable debris (sticks, rotting leaves, grass clippings, pet feces, and the like) has an impact on the marine environment, for in decaying, organic matter steals dissolved oxygen from the water. Far more insidious, however, is nondegradable debris, and in particular plastics—fishing line, six-pack rings, plastic bags, straws and cups, even tiny resin pellets—which entangle or are ingested by tens of thousands of marine animals each year.

Too often, polluted runoff is generated either because people are not aware of how their own actions contribute to the problem, or because they maintain that one person's actions are inconsequential and have no signficant impact one way or the other. When considering oil and the damage it does to the environment, for example, many people conjure up images of huge tankers, their hulls ripped open, releasing millions of gallons of murky black liquid into an aquatic environment. But every year, more oil, either from leaky cars or improper disposal, travels into the nation's waters through municipal storm drains than all the oil spilled from the Exxon *Valdez*. And a single gallon of motor oil can do plenty of damage, creating a slick eight acres in size and contaminating about one million gallons of drinking water in the process. In other words, one person's actions—flicking a cigarette butt, applying a toxic pesticide, or throwing out a gallon of used motor oil—are precisely what do count.

SOURCES OF POLLUTED RUNOFF

The types of pollutants found in a waterway are usually a direct reflection of how the adjacent land is used. The Chesapeake Bay, for example, which is downstream from a heavily farmed region, is prone to nutrient overenrichment. Santa Monica Bay, on the other hand, whose watershed drains from a heavily urbanized and industrialized area, is heavily laden with toxins and debris. Below are several types of land use that are often associated with polluted runoff.

Agriculture
In the United States, agriculture is considered far and away the greatest source of polluted runoff. Certain farming techniques, such as planting crops all the way to stream edges or deep-plowing croplands, make cultivated areas extremely prone to erosion. Eroded soil not only degrades streams through sedimentation but can also carry toxins from heavy applications of pesticides and herbicides, as well as phosphorus and nitrogen from fertilizers. Large quantities of livestock manure, if not properly contained, also wash into streams and rivers with every rainfall.

Logging

Clear-cutting a forest and creating mud roads to transport timber are both recipes for erosion. And once a forest canopy has been stripped away, streams becomes unnaturally warm, prone to heavy alga growth, and inhospitable to the aquatic plants and animals that normally inhabit them.

Hydromodification

Channeling, damming, dredging, or changing the course of a waterway all cause severe sedimentation and all of the problems associated with it. Hydromodification also tends to increase the velocity of water in a waterway, producing a profound scouring effect.

Marinas

Construction of marinas can destroy valuable wetland and estuarine areas. And because marinas are usually located in waters that are poorly flushed, toxins found in boat paints, gasoline and oil, and bacteria and organic matter from improperly treated boat bilge tend to accumulate in the water.

Urbanization

The development of natural areas has a profound and long-lasting effect on both inland and coastal waterways and deserves more than a quick look. A whole constellation of problems, ranging from deforestation to increased human population, is associated with urbanization.

Construction, for example, can be quite damaging to nearby waterways. Whenever it rains, one acre of land cleared for construction can release into nearby waterways about one hundred times the amount of soil that would be lost off one acre of well-managed farmland, and as much as a thousand times the amount that would be lost from an acre of forest.

Paving over an area also has its consequences. In a natural environment, soil acts as a filter, removing toxins and other pollutants as the water percolates through it. The water, in turn, replenishes underwater aquifers and seeps slowly into nearby ponds, lakes, and streams. But in areas where the ground has been capped with cement, asphalt, or any other impervious surface, rainwater never reaches the soil. Instead, it washes over rooftops and gushes through downspouts; runs over sidewalks, roads, and parking lots; and pours into culverts and storm drains, all the while picking up plastic bags, cigarette butts, toxic residues, grit, road salt, and the like. Rich in pollutants, it shoots through the storm-drain system, which funnels it into the nearest waterway.

In a heavily paved area, waterways that would otherwise receive a slow, steady flow of filtered water are instead bombarded by torrents of fast-moving, highly polluted water after each rainfall. And during dry times, with nothing to sustain them, they often run dry. In response to this wildly fluctuating water flow, their banks quickly erode, and aquatic life slowly dies off.

Another problem associated with urban areas is the wastewater disposal method known as a combined sewer system. In some cities, an infrastructure of underground water tunnels combines the sewage lines—which carry water to a treatment plant—with the storm-drain system. Under normal conditions, this means that both residential sewage and street runoff are routed to the treatment plant. But when heavy rains threaten to overload the system, water is diverted around the treatment plant and sent straight into the nearest waterway, accompanied by household toxins, raw sewage, debris such as syringes and condoms, and anything else that has been flushed down a toilet or has washed down a drain.

MONITORING FOR CLEANER WATERS

Estuaries, which provide vitally important spawning and nursery grounds, abundant food, and protective habitat for a whole host of aquatic life, are at the receiving end of just about every sort of pollution imaginable, point source and nonpoint source alike. Street runoff, nutrients from gardens and lawns, eroded soil, industrial discharge thick with toxins—all of these accompany fresh water as it travels toward the ocean. Estuaries do receive a regular influx of seawater, but because they are by definition semi-enclosed bodies of water, only a limited amount of pollution gets washed out to sea with each outgoing tide.

Before an estuary can be cleaned up, the offending pollutants need to be identified and the damage assessed. Taking the pulse of an estuary, or indeed of any body of water, is the job of a huge team of citizens throughout the country who call themselves volunteer monitors.

Monitoring a body of water may mean measuring certain characteristics, or parameters, each of which describes one aspect of the water's health. Salinity, temperature, and water clarity are common parameters. But monitoring can also mean assessing flora or fauna—sea grass, fish, or shellfish, for example—that normally make their home in the water. In deciding what to test for, a monitoring association starts by looking at what questions need to be answered, and designs the program accordingly. If, for example, members suspect that coastal waters are contaminated from nearby septic tanks, they will most likely sample the water for fecal coliform, a group of bacteria found in human and animal wastes. If algae seems to be growing out of control, monitors will measure dissolved oxygen. And if large quantities of mud appear to be washing from an upstream construction project into an estuary, water clarity will certainly be tested.

While some of the monitoring tests are fairly simple, others can be quite painstaking. Coliform testing, for example, requires that a water sample be gathered in a sterile container, then taken to a lab and sucked through a special type of filter that separates out any invisible bacteria. The filter is placed in growing media and incubated overnight, so that by the next morning the bacteria are large enough to be counted. The test for water clarity, on the other hand, is a model of simplicity: Volunteers lower a specialized disk into the water and note the depth at which it disappears.

MONITORING'S GROWING POPULARITY

Volunteer environmental monitoring is not, of course, limited to estuaries. Its roots, in fact, are planted in the nation's streams, lakes, and rivers. Save Our Streams, started in Maryland in 1969 when citizens became concerned about mud pollution from construction sites, represented the first time that volunteers, rather than paid scientific staff, tested and cleaned up the waters. Lake- and river-monitoring groups slowly followed suit, but it was not until the 1980s that the first estuarine programs got underway. (Estuaries, because of their complex interplay of salt water and fresh water, are somewhat more challenging to monitor than lakes and rivers.) Ocean monitoring was initiated in 1984, when a small group of Malibu surfers began testing the surf zone for bacterial contamination and disseminating their test results to the general public. Today, the Surfrider Foundation's Blue Water Task Force is a highly respected water-monitoring program operated by Surfrider volunteers and members on both the Pacific and Atlantic coasts.

Sometimes, it is an environmental crisis that precipitates the formation of a monitoring group. In 1987, for example, Maine's Damariscotta River, traditionally a healthy, bountiful waterway where aquaculture and lobstering flourished, was closed to all shellfishing activity due to bacterial contamination. Maine's Clean Water Program was established, and soon members had begun sampling the water, identifying pollution "hot spots," and cleaning up whatever sources they could identify. The program was successful enough that after two years, members decided to offer support and training to others interested in starting their own program. By 1995, Maine's Clean Water Program had grown to include twenty-two monitoring programs and more than a thousand volunteers. And while shellfish contamination was what initially motivated the formation of these groups, the monitoring, it turned out, was to be a springboard for a host of other environmental advocacy and education projects: Monitoring associations throughout the state have carried out coastal cleanups, produced educational videos, and taken on erosion-control projects. One association even lobbied—successfully—for funding to built a state-of-the-art, environmentally sound sewage-treatment plant.

The popularity of monitoring in Maine is mirrored in a dramatic growth in the movement nationwide. Consider that when the first national directory of volunteer monitoring was published in 1988, it listed some eighty-eight groups, scattered among twenty-four states. By 1993, more than five hundred groups could be counted, representing forty-five states and the District of Columbia. Today, literally tens of thousands of volunteers are dipping nets into streams to examine macroinvertebrate (that is, bug) populations, sampling water near outfall pipes to measure toxin levels, checking shellfish populations for sewage-related bacteria, and employing a whole range of techniques—some sophisticated, others fairly simple—to assess water quality.

And, armed with the knowledge that pollution is generated from so many disparate sources, monitoring groups are increasingly interested in evaluating entire watersheds and the ways the land that drains into the water is used—testing, for example, not just a single tidal pool, but the pool, the freshwater streams that feed into it, and the coastal waters that flow in with each tide. By examining a complete watershed, monitors can not only measure the pollution in an area, but often pinpoint its source as well.

Hand in hand with the growth of volunteer monitoring has come its rise in credibility. For many years, federal, state, and local regulatory agencies remained skeptical that citizens, rather than paid scientific staff, could accurately collect and analyze scientific data. For many groups, establishing credibilty has been an uphill battle, achieved only after proving that they could generate precise, accurate data, year after year (see "The Salt Pond Watchers," below). Moreover, regulatory agencies, feeling the sting of budget and staff cutbacks, in many cases no longer have the resources to monitor the waters themselves. As a result, many of these agencies have come to rely on the steady stream of dedicated citizens who offer their monitoring services for free. Often, government agencies show their support of the volunteer associations by performing analyses of water samples at little or no cost. And more than half of all monitoring groups report that their data are used by either state or federal agencies.

STILL A GRASSROOTS MOVEMENT

Volunteer monitoring has a lot to recommend it. Perhaps most importantly, it provides a constructive, hands-on way for people to help improve the waters near where they live. Volunteers also have the satisfaction of knowing that their own role, no matter how small, will contribute to a far larger effort: One volunteer might sample the waters of a nearby marsh only once a month, but when his or her data is combined with the data of nine other volunteers, the results are likely to be taken seriously by local officials, and may ultimately affect important land-use decisions. Writing a check to a national environmental organization simply cannot provide this sort of reward.

Volunteer monitoring, in fact, remains essentially a home-grown movement (an average monitoring association numbers only twenty-five people, and has a budget of about four thousand dollars) whose workers are motivated by a desire to clean up *their* waters, the places where they and their families swim, sail, fish, clam, water-ski, relax, and observe wildlife. As Eleanor Ely, editor of *The Volunteer Monitor* newsletter, observes, "These people are watching waters that they know personally."

And identifying exactly what ails the water is only part of the reason volunteers find their work so satisfying. When asked what they consider to be the single most important use of their data, volunteer programs often cite "education"— spreading an awareness about the value of their waters—which takes place not only at town meetings but in conversations among neighbors and friends, in the classroom, and at cocktail parties. As Delaware Riverkeeper Cynthia Poten describes it:

> *The explosion of interest in volunteer monitoring translates into a lot more people actively committed to protecting their local environment. People who are investing time and energy in monitoring have a stronger motivation to speak out on behalf of a resource—to attend municipal meetings, comment at public hearings, and write elected officials—especially since they are also armed with reliable information on local conditions.*

Monitoring has something else in its favor: It can usually be fit into a normal, overly busy life. The work can be broken down into discrete tasks, and most of these can be scheduled ahead of time, which means that someone with a limited amount of time to contribute can still join in. It also brings together people within a community who might otherwise have nothing in common, people who do not necessarily consider themselves hard-core environmentalists but who share a desire to protect a local natural resource. A typical Maine monitoring association, for example, might include those who make their living harvesting shellfish, representatives of the local land trust, students, town officials, and other assorted volunteers.

Students, in fact, have added an exciting new dimension to the monitoring movement. Well over half of the programs surveyed in 1993 reported collaborating with middle- and high-school students, while more than 40 percent said they worked with elementary-level students. One program, based in Camden, Maine, is entirely run by high-school students. And thanks to an innovative program called GREEN (Global Rivers Environmental Education Network), based in Ann Arbor, Michigan, educators and teachers have been able to implement and sustain monitoring and watershed education programs in some twenty-five thousand classrooms throughout the world.

THE APPEAL OF MONITORING

Monitoring may not, however, be suited to everyone. With some exceptions (see "The Keeper Programs," page 61), volunteer monitoring is steady, methodical work, and brings about changes that are rarely dramatic. A successful endeavor may cause the state to open or close shellfish beds, or induce town officials to upgrade a local sewage-treatment plant, but it will not usually precipitate a lawsuit or lead to the closing of a major industrial facility. In most situations, volunteer monitors achieve their goals by passing information on to community and state leaders—working, in other words, *within* the system to restore the quality of their lake, stream, or bay. "Monitors are not usually the type of people who want to wave the red flag at City Hall," says Virginia Lee, founder of the Rhode Island Salt Pond Watchers Program. "They are more like the postman"—persistently carrying out their task despite the obstacles standing in their way. "Monitoring is a slow, patient, un-flashy type of exercise. You want results, but you go into it knowing that often it's going to be a long-term endeavor."

GETTING STARTED

For anyone interested in initiating a volunteer monitoring program, here are some suggestions from the experts. "Find some models and find some partners," suggests Eleanor Ely of *The Volunteer Monitor*. A good source of models is *The National Directory of Volunteer Environmental Monitoring Programs* (see below). As for partners, hook up with a source of expert help: a university laboratory, another local monitoring group, a state or local environmental agency, or even a program such as Maine's Clean Water Program that specializes in getting new groups up and running. Try to find others in the community who share your concerns about the waterway you plan to monitor. And once you have committed yourself to initiating a program, make sure that the questions that led you to monitor in the first place continue to guide you as you design the program.

Three publications in particular will be useful to someone new to the movement: the Environmental Protection Agency's *Volunteer Estuary Monitoring: A Methods Manual* (also available are a methods manual for lake monitoring and an upcoming manual on stream monitoring); *The National Directory of Volunteer Environmental Monitoring Programs,* Fourth Edition, also published by the E.P.A.; and *The Volunteer Monitor,* an excellent biannual newsletter that covers such salient topics as fundraising, building credibility, and developing technical field expertise. The monitoring programs described below, all of which focus on coastal and estuarine waterways, reveal some of the strengths, as well as the challenges, of the burgeoning monitoring movement.

THE SALT POND WATCHERS

Rhode Island Pond Watchers

Scientists may call them coastal lagoons or near-shore estuaries, but for those who live near them and know them well, the shallow bodies of water lying behind Rhode Island's barrier beaches are better known as salt ponds. Eight such ponds are the site of one of the country's oldest estuarine monitoring projects.

Salt ponds are tremendously productive estuarine systems. Besides supporting large populations of scallops, oysters, quahogs, and soft-shell clams, Rhode Island's ponds serve as spawning grounds for winter flounder, as nurseries for juvenile striped bass and bluefish, and as home to American eels and numerous fish species. Their location makes them the first stop for all of the polluted runoff that finds its inevitable way to the ocean; in the words of one scientist, salt ponds are "the sentinels of the coast," able to sound the alarm for water-quality deterioration before the pollutants ever arrive at the open ocean.

Rhode Island's salt ponds are as vital economically as they are ecologically. Boating, swimming, birding, water-skiing, and commercial and recreational fishing and clamming make the ponds quite popular year-round, and in the summer, an estimated 165,000 visitors may flock to their shores each day. Not surprisingly, residential development near the ponds has skyrocketed, precipitating bacterial contamination and nutrient enrichment, the dual problems associated with homeowner septic systems.

The Salt Pond Watcher Program was formed in 1985 by local residents concerned about the ponds' declining health. As is typical of monitoring groups, these volunteers represented a variety of backgrounds, among them contractor, locksmith, pediatrician, banker, university professor, and elementary-school teacher. Many were retired. The first year, forty-five volunteers began sampling six sites (three for bacteria and three for nutrients) in each of the eight ponds. But, as the Salt Pond Watchers learned at the outset, their main hurdle was not so much learning to monitor as making their voices heard.

"We were one of the early coastal monitoring programs," says Virginia Lee, of the Coastal Resources Center and Rhode Island Sea Grant, University of Rhode Island, and founder of the program, "and the state was at first quite suspicious about whether our data could be reliable." The Salt Pond Watchers decided to create a program that adhered so closely to the state's own methods and standards (the state, at the time, was carrying out a limited amount of monitoring of its own) that there could be no logical reason for disregarding the volunteers' data. And, from the start, they established an excellent track record.

Nonetheless, for two years the state's Department of Environmental Management (DEM) remained guarded about accepting Pond Watcher data. "But by the third year," says Lee, "they were finding our data so useful that they asked us to expand our program and sample at all their stations—which we did. The bacterial contamination, it turned out, was enough for DEM to close portions of three of the ponds to shellfishing."

In their first decade of operation, the Pond Watchers have proven their worth time and again, not only in charting long-term trends in the ponds' health, but by taking advantage of "windows of opportunity" to make important observations that a less vigilant group might have missed. In 1987, for example, when a gravel road was temporarily installed over an inlet that connected one of the ponds to the ocean, effectively sealing the pond off from the ocean, the Pond Watchers' analysis pointed to skyrocketing levels of nutrients—confirming a long-held fear that the pond was serving as the local dumping ground for nutrient runoff. The data was dramatic enough to alert both local and state officials, who responded by collaborating on legislation for improved siting and construction standards for septic systems, which will go a long way toward ensuring cleaner water in the ponds.

Falmouth's Pond Watchers

Falmouth, Massachusetts, near the base of Cape Cod, is the site of another group of salt ponds. Like their counterparts in

Rhode Island, these ponds are a hub of activity for both year-round residents and summer visitors, and feel acutely the pressures from nearby residential and commercial development. In summer, just when conditions in the ponds make them especially sensitive to stress, the town's population of about twenty-five thousand triples in size—which translates into three times as many people clamming, fishing, boating, swimming, and sending their discharge into pond waters. Helping the ponds to withstand these pressures, however, are a group of more than sixty-five volunteers who call themselves the Pond Watchers and a small team of scientists at the Woods Hole Oceanographic Institution.

At least four times each summer, at more than thirty sites throughout the ponds, the volunteers measure temperature and dissolved oxygen, collect samples for nutrient analysis, and pass everything on to the Woods Hole scientists. They, in turn, after analyzing the samples and interpreting the data, experiment with innovative solutions to the nutrient problem. And, on an as-needed basis, they also advise the town of Falmouth on methods for managing the ponds—suggesting, for example, that a particular pond could or could not withstand the runoff likely to result from a proposed development.

What distinguishes the Pond Watchers from most other monitoring groups is that their mission is to gather research-quality data—quantitative information that can safely be incorporated into scientific research and used for environmental management. To encourage their efforts, Woods Hole scientists Brian Howes and Dale Goehringer provide the volunteers with extensive training, not only teaching them monitoring techniques, but also including a crash course of sorts about salt-pond ecology. Long before they dip a sampling bottle in the water, volunteers learn about the watershed that supports the ponds, how humans affect the watershed system, and how and when the system becomes taxed to the point at which it can no longer function. All of this, says Goehringer, has an impact. "The volunteers take extraordinary care in their collecting," she says, "and become very dedicated to the cause. They also become very astute in noticing changes taking place. If, for example, there's an alga bloom on one of the ponds, we get a dozen calls from the volunteers. They're the eyes, ears, and noses of the ponds."

All of those involved in the collaboration have benefited. The town, whose allure to visitors is closely tied to the health of its waters, recives a steady flow of recommendations about how best to care for the ponds and also enjoys the support of a motivated and mobilized citizens' group. Volunteers have the satisfaction of seeing their data used to improve the health of the ponds. And the scientists, equipped with a valuable stream of data that would be nearly impossible to gather on their own, are able to work toward solutions to the ongoing challenge of salt-pond pollution.

THE KEEPER PROGRAMS

Most volunteer monitoring efforts are spawned when a group of people become disgruntled about a waterway and decide to do something about it. The Keeper programs—Baykeepers, Riverkeepers, and Soundkeepers—are different, for at the heart of each program is a single person, a "Keeper," charged with the formidable task of protecting a particular river, sound, or bay. And while most volunteer monitoring programs chart long-term trends in water quality, Keeper programs assume a direct and often confrontational role as advocates for their waterways. Not content merely to measure salinity, temperature, and the like, the Keepers, with the help of small staffs and eager volunteers, use investigative, monitoring, and legal skills to bring environmental violators to justice.

Bob Boyle, president of the Hudson River Fishermen's Association, conceived of the idea of a Riverkeeper after reading about the keepers in Britain—men whose job it was to care for privately owned rivers and streams rich in trout and salmon. If someone were given the job of protecting a river on behalf of the public interest rather than for a private landowner, Boyle reasoned, waterways such as the Hudson might benefit tremendously. In 1981, the Hudson River Fishermen's Association hired its first Keeper. His task: to protect the ecological integrity of the Hudson and its watershed.

In 1983, a man named John Cronin took on the position of Hudson Riverkeeper. Cronin's first case got the program off to a spectacular start. After receiving a tip about some tankers in the Hudson River, he and his team spent six months carrying out nighttime surveillance, water monitoring, and background investigation. Eventually they pieced together a highly illegal scenario: Exxon tankers, it turned out, were regularly traveling up to a freshwater area of the river, discharging tons of oily, toxinladen seawater, then filling their tanks with fresh water which they transported to the island of Aruba for use in one of the company's oil refineries. Exxon, when confronted with the evidence amassed against it, settled out of court to the tune of $2 million—$500,000 going to Riverkeeper, and $1.5 million earmarked for the Hudson River Improvement Fund.

The Hudson Riverkeeper has continued to wage war on behalf of the river. In 1987 Robert F. Kennedy Jr., in partnership with John Cronin, established the Pace University Law School Environmental Law Clinic, whose law students are only too willing to research cases and file suits on behalf of the organization. By 1995 the Hudson Riverkeeper could boast of having won more than seventy cases against environmental violators.

Delaware Riverkeeper Cynthia Poten has taken a different tack in caring for the thirteen thousand square miles of land that make up the Delaware River watershed. Poten's advocacy program centers on empowering citizens to become effective stewards for what she calls their "home waters"—their piece of the watershed. As part of this mission, Poten assembles local task forces whose members assume responsibility for the health of a specific stream, lake, or section of river. Riverkeeper staff then train task force members in the nuts-and-bolts skills involved in environmental advocacy—everything from identifying water problems to raising money, writing press releases, holding news conferences, and recruiting volunteers to plant trees for a streambank reservation.

Some of the Keeper programs are almost legendary in their willingness to do battle. San Francisco BayKeeper Mike Herz* has acquired a reputation for his blunt, often confrontational approach to polluters. "The Keeper's self-appointed task," says Herz, "is to find people who are breaking the law and do something about it."

In Herz's view, there is no scarcity of laws designed to ensure healthy waters; the problem stems from the fact that they are not always taken seriously. Under the Clean Water Act, industries discharging wastewater are required to have permits regulating the concentration of toxins they release. But government agencies responsible for enforcing these regulations have neither the time nor the resources to monitor all of the dischargers.

The role of the San Francisco BayKeeper, as Herz sees it, is to fill this void in enforcement, first by making life unpleasant for the polluters, but also by pressuring enforcement agencies to take a tougher stance on violators. On a day-to-day basis, Herz and his staff, along with an able army of volunteers, survey sites of suspected illegal activity and collect water samples to make sure companies are complying with their pollution permits. They also carry out detective work of a sort, gathering evidence that will link what goes on inside an industrial facility (what chemicals, for example, are used during manufacturing processes) with what winds up in the water near the company's discharge pipe.

Those who volunteer with the San Francisco BayKeeper seem to relish the organization's somewhat maverick approach to environmental monitoring, and to enjoy the action-oriented nature of the work: walking the shore in search of a drainage pipe, paddling a kayak alongside a freighter to take water samples, surveying sites of suspected illegal activity from their own airplane or helicopter.

But bringing polluters to justice can be an involved and drawn-out process. One of Herz's favorite cases, for example, took three years to resolve. The project got under way when BayKeeper received a tip about some dredging that appeared to be going on near a bay shipyard. First, the organization sent out a kayaker who surveyed the shipyard under cover of night (a volunteer Herz refers to as "our secret weapon"). The kayaker had no trouble locating the activity, and photographed workers dredging in highly contaminated sediment. The workers were dumping the dredged sediment right back into the bay, releasing into the underwater environment a host of long-buried toxins. Water samples subsequently taken at the site revealed high levels of copper, zinc, lead, and a now-banned chemical called tributyltin (once used to keep barnacles off boats), that is highly toxic to shellfish.

BayKeeper reported its findings to the appropriate regulatory agency, but when the agency responded by proposing a mere six-thousand-dollar fine, payable as a tax-deductible, charitable contribution, BayKeeper went into high gear and initiated a campaign to bring about a more appropriate punishment. The organization called on another of its volunteers, a former employee of the shipyard, who produced an affidavit explaining how the company had tried to keep the dredging secret. A boatload of reporters was then transported out to the dredging site, where Herz described in detail the alleged crime. And, to make sure the case would be given the attention it deserved, BayKeeper alerted the Environmental Protection Agency's Criminal Investigation Unit. As a result of the E.P.A.'s investigation, the U.S. Attorney's Office indicted the company and its president and vice president on forty-five violations of the Clean Water Act. Both officers were sent to jail. The company was also heavily fined for violations of the Resource Conservation and Recovery Act. BayKeeper estimates that in the few months during which the dredging took place, the equivalent of 640 dump-truck loads of contaminated sediment were reintroduced into San Francisco Bay. Since 1983, when John Cronin began patrolling the waters of the Hudson River, more than a dozen Keeper programs have sprung up to protect waters from Alaska's Cook Inlet to Atlanta's Chattahoochee River. For the concept of a Keeper— someone entrusted with the care of an entire waterway—is an appealing one. "The Keeper," says Cynthia Poten, "is really a symbol for personal stewardship and individual responsibility. The Keeper is one individual who says, 'I'm going to take care of this water body. I'm going to make a difference.'"

MONITORING MORE THAN THE WATER

Biomonitoring—monitoring the living organisms of an ecosystem—can be undertaken for any number of reasons. A particular plant or animal might be monitored because it is highly valued and imperiled, or, conversely, because it poses a threat to the existing ecosystem (the most ready example being the zebra mussel). In many cases, the health of an organism, or community of organisms, provides some useful insights into the water's health. In streams throughout the country, for example, volunteers monitor populations of snails, worms, and insect larvae collectively referred to as macroinvertebrates. A volunteer dips a net into the stream, pulls out the tiny, squirming life forms, and identifies and counts them. A healthy complement of creatures including mayflies, stoneflies, and caddis flies—all pollution-sensitive species—is a good sign. Finding nothing but leeches, midges, and aquatic worms, on the other hand—all of which are notably sewage-tolerant—indicates a real problem.

In coastal and estuarine areas, biomonitoring can involve

virtually any species. The animals and plants do not even need to be alive to be counted: In the state of Washington, volunteers with Adopt-A-Beach walk sections of the shore along Puget Sound and the outer coast in search of dead shorebirds. Each bird is duly recorded by the volunteer, and its species, maturity level, and probable cause of death noted. The information is used to establish baseline data on shorebird mortality so that when a catastrophic event such as an oil spill occurs, the effect on shorebird mortality can be accurately gauged.

The SAV Hunt

Submerged aquatic vegetation (SAV), once considered a nuisance because of its tendency to become tangled in boat propellers and detract from the aesthetics of a sandy-bottomed swimming area, is in fact one of the most valuable of estuarine resources. The more than a dozen species of SAV (also referred to as bay grass) found in the shallower waters of the Chesapeake Bay and its tidal tributaries provide vital habitat for a wide range of estuarine life. Barnacles and scallop larvae survive by adhering to the plants' leaves and stems; juvenile bluefish, minnows, and molting blue crabs find shelter from predators in its midst, while waterfowl, both resident and migratory, dine on its roots, tubers, and seed heads. As well, innumerable other underwater animals benefit from the oxygen produced through the grasses' photosynthesis.

Survival of the SAV, however, is tied closely to the overall health of the bay. In fact, many consider the bay grasses to be the single best indicator of the Chesapeake's water quality. Scientists estimate that as much as 90 percent of the beds have been lost as a result of sediment and nutrient pollution. (More recently, however, the SAV beds have started to make a heartening comeback in response to a huge baywide restoration project.)

It is no wonder that those concerned about the health of the bay like to keep a very close watch on the SAV beds. And it is here, in the SAV monitoring, that volunteers can play an important role. Each year the U.S. Fish and Wildlife Service, with the support of several state and federal agencies, carries out an aerial survey of the bay, photographing the dark spots in the water that appear to be SAV beds. The next spring, about a hundred volunteers from Maryland, Virginia, and Pennsylvania receive maps reflecting the survey results. In shallow-draft boats or by wading along the shoreline, they proceed on a "ground-truthing" mission—verifying the presence of beds that appear in the photographs, identifying the grasses, and noting the presence of any beds missed by the camera.

For volunteers, most of whom live near the Chesapeake and have for decades watched in frustration as conditions have deteriorated, there is the satisfaction of knowing they are helping to document the health of the bay's waters. On occasion, volunteers have also spotted beds that were missed by aerial observation, then lobbied to alter development plans (in one case, the expansion of a marina) in order to protect the beds. Perhaps most importantly, the SAV Hunt gets volunteers out into the waters of the bay, where they have a chance to observe the wildlife living in, on, and around the grasses. They, in turn, become stronger advocates for the SAV, and are equipped to educate others about just how vital the grasses' survival is to the future of the Chesapeake.

Coral Watch

Coral Watch, a program sponsored jointly by The Nature Conservancy and the National Oceanic and Atmospheric Administration (NOAA), gives highly trained divers the opportunity to help save coral reefs in the Florida Keys National Marine Sanctuary. "We know the reefs aren't what they were twenty years ago," says Mary Enstrom, the program's volunteer coordinator, "but what the divers are doing is documenting precisely how they're changing."

During the dives, volunteers identify and carefully inspect the corals, sponges, and algae in designated reef locations throughout the sanctuary. A daylong training session at a nearby community college is required for new volunteers.

Valerie Herbert, a professional diver from The Living Seas Program at Walt Disney World's Epcot Center who regularly travels down to the Keys for long weekends of volunteer diving, says the program has heightened her awareness of the kinds of dangers reefs are facing today. "These corals are so delicate," she explains, "that the touch of a diver's fin or the careless toss of an anchor can destroy decades of growth in only seconds." Another potential danger for the reefs, says Herbert, is agricultural runoff, which can create alga blooms that block light vital to the coral's survival.

The data gathered by the divers is incorporated into a marine data bank and disseminated to scientists and coastal zone managers, and—perhaps giving the greatest satisfaction to the divers—it is also at the heart of an ambitious plan to create a sort of underwater zoning, one that would balance the public's use of these waters against the needs of the plants and animals inhabiting them.

SURFRIDER FOUNDATION AND THE
BLUE WATER TASK FORCE

The organization that has taken the lead in coastal water monitoring had its inauspicious beginnings on a Malibu beach just over a decade ago. When a handful of surfers grew frustrated at seeing their favorite waters turned unsavory shades of brown and gray, routinely paddling through debris, and coming down with everything from sore throats to skin rashes and dysentery, they formed a small coastal advocacy group called the Surfrider Foundation. In its first decade, Surfrider has evolved into a formidable force whose twenty-five-thousand-plus members—"anyone who has experienced the magic of a perfect wave or the pleasure of a sandy beach . . ."—wage wars on behalf of beaches, waves, and water quality.

Flying in the face of the stereotype that paints surfers as laid back and wholly self-absorbed, Surfrider enjoys a reputation as an impassioned and effective group of environmental activists. The organization's thirty chapters, which operate entirely on a volunteer basis, carry out projects ranging from storm-drain stenciling to beach cleanups and natural dune restorations. Campaigns are fought to ensure beach access, to prevent damaging coastal development, and even to extend outfall pipes so that polluted waters will be piped out beyond the range of surfers and swimmers. Through a program called "Respect the Beach," Surfrider also ventures into California classrooms to teach about ocean ecology, environmental stewardship, and beach safety.

In 1991, in conjunction with the Environmental Protection Agency, Surfrider won the second largest suit ever filed on behalf of the Clean Water Act. The suit charged two large paper pulp mills, located in northern California's Humboldt County, of discharging some forty million gallons of dioxin- and chlorine-laced water a day into prime surfing waters. It is something of a source of pride to the Surfrider Foundation that one of the mills, after losing the suit, overhauled its paper-production practices and several years later became the first mill in the country to produce chlorine-free paper.

But filing a lawsuit is usually considered a last resort for Surfrider, which prefers using other methods to show the world that, in the words of one member, "we don't want to surf or swim in sewage." In 1993, for example, more than forty Surfrider members climbed on their boards and headed out into frigid New Jersey waters, staging a "paddle-out protest" to alert the public about offshore dioxin dumping.

It is perhaps little wonder that the Surfrider Foundation spearheaded the first standardized water-quality monitoring program for coastal waters. The "Blue Water Task Force" (BWTF), as the program is called, relies on the fact that hundreds of Surfrider members already spend inordinate amounts of time in the waves, and are only too willing to dip a test tube into troubled waters as part of an effort to clean them up.

Often, testing is initiated in response to a particular problem—when swimmers at a particular beach, for example, complain of recurring ear and nose infections. If testing reveals high bacterium levels, Surfrider representatives approach local water-quality boards and county health departments with their data. "We function as a kind of red flag," says Ed Mazzarella, Surfrider chapter program director, "that lets the agencies know that there's a problem out there." In a couple of Surfrider chapters, where testing is carried out at a fairly high level of sophistication, test results are also disseminated to the general public on a weekly basis, either through local newspaper and radio announcements or through a water-quality hotline.

If local agencies refuse to respond to the test results, the local Surfrider chapter may take matters into its own hands and post signs in the area, warning surfers and swimmers of potentially dangerous conditions. But whenever possible, the Blue Water Task Force opts for a nonadversarial, proactive approach toward water-quality problems. The point of the program is to clean up the waters, says Mazzarella, "not to point fingers."

FOR MORE INFORMATION

A good introduction to polluted runoff is provided by:

Luck Isn't Enough: The Fight for Clean Water, *an easy-to-understand, twelve-minute videotape.* **To borrow or purchase the video, call or write:**

NEW YORK SEA GRANT EXTENSION PROGRAM
125 Nassau Hall
SUNY at Stony Brook
Stony Brook, NY 11794-5002
(516) 632-8730

All water-quality related publications from the Environmental Protection Agency may be obtained by contacting:

NATIONAL VOLUNTEER MONITORING COORDINATOR
U.S. Environmental Protection Agency
Office of Water 4503F
Washington, D.C. 20460
(202) 260-7018

Monitoring organizations discussed in this chapter may be found in the E.P.A.'s *National Directory of Volunteer Environmental Monitoring Programs.*

Subscriptions to The Volunteer Monitor *newsletter are free.* To be added to the mailing list, write to:

ELEANOR ELY
Editor
The Volunteer Monitor
1318 Masonic Avenue
San Francisco, CA 94117

The existing *Keeper* programs are as follows:

SAN FRANCISCO BAYKEEPER
Fort Mason
Building A
San Francisco, CA 94123
(415) 567-4401

DELAWARE RIVERKEEPER
P.O. Box 753
Lambertville, NJ 08530
(609) 397-4410

LONG ISLAND SOUNDKEEPER
P.O. Box 4058
East Norwalk, CT 06855
(800) 933-SOUN

SAN DIEGO SOUNDKEEPER
P.O. Box 82045
San Diego, CA 92138-2045
(619) 299-4484

CASCO BAYKEEPER
P.O. Box 7758
Portland, ME 04112
(207) 799-8574

HUDSON RIVERKEEPER
P.O. Box 130
Garrison, NY 10524
(800) 21-RIVER

NY-NJ HARBOR BAYKEEPER
American Littoral Society
Sandy Hook
Highlands, NJ 07732
(908) 291-0055

SANTA MONICA BAYKEEPER
13900 Tahiti Way
Slip A-231
P.O. Box 10096
Marina del Rey, CA 90295
(800) HELP-BAY

NARRAGANSETT BAYKEEPER
Save the Bay
434 Smith Street
Providence, RI 02908
(401) 272-3540

NEUSE RIVERKEEPER
P.O. Box 15451
New Bern, NC 28561
(929) 637-7972

UPPER CHATTAHOOCHEE RIVERKEEPER
P.O. Box 7338
Atlanta, GA 30357-0338
(404) 816-9888

LOWER CHATTAHOOCHEE
RIVERKEEPER
P.O. Box 1492
Columbus, GA 31902
(706) 322-5608

PUGET SOUNDKEEPER ALLIANCE
1415 West Dravis
Seattle, WA 98119
(206) 286-1309

MAINE'S CLEAN WATER PROGRAM
University of Maine Cooperative
Extension
375 Main Street
Rockland, ME 04841
(207) 594-2104

For information on the Blue Water Task Force, contact:

SURFRIDER FOUNDATION
122 South El Camino Real #67
San Clemente, CA 92672
(714) 492-8170

*Editor's Note: In late 1995, Mike Herz relinquished his role of
San Francisco BayKeeper and assumed the title of Keeper Emeritus.

Protecting Coastal Wildlife

For many people interested in coastal issues, it may not be enough to join in an annual coastal cleanup or even to assess the health of the local estuary. These individuals are passionately interested in coastal and marine wildlife, especially those species that are threatened by problems such as coastal development, polluted waters, or debris-strewn shores. They may have seen pictures of seal pups, their necks encircled in plastic nets. They may have read about mass die-offs of dolphins. They may never have seen a sea turtle or a manatee, but they want to do something to help ensure that these animals will survive well into the next century and beyond.

Fortunately, there is plenty that citizens can do for the protection and preservation of coastal and marine wildlife. The first step is to find out what organizations are working on behalf of these species and to support them—by contributing financially, by volunteering in any sort of capacity, by writing letters to legislators, and, most importantly, by helping to educate the public. In Monterey, California, for example, volunteers with Friends of the Sea Otter's Otter Spotter program post themselves along the coast with telescopes, encouraging visitors to view these highly engaging creatures and learn a bit about what threatens them. In Massachusetts, volunteers with the Coastal Waterbird Program spend their summer days on barrier beaches, explaining to beachgoers why plovers and terns deserve a quiet, safe section of coastline.

Working on behalf of coastal wildlife does not always mean working one-on-one with animals. In fact, approaching coastal wildlife can in some instances be quite dangerous—for both humans and animals. Under the Marine Mammal Protection Act of 1972, for example, citizens, unless authorized through the Marine Mammal Stranding Network, are forbidden to harass, touch, or hurt a marine mammal, even if the animal appears injured or sick. Seal and otter pups found alone on the beach should be left alone. A beached dolphin should not be pushed back into the ocean. Children should not be placed on or near an elephant seal so that their picture can be snapped. If an animal appears sick, injured, or abandoned, the local police should be called.

Much of the hands-on humanitarian work involving coastal or marine wildlife should be left to professionals. Nonetheless, citizens can do much to support both conservation and humanitarian efforts. Whale enthusiasts may not be able to work directly with whales, for example, but may find great satisfaction in helping to fund researchers who have taken on the challenge of disentangling whales from commercial fishing nets. On the other hand, volunteers are essential to certain types of animal rescue and rehabilitation. Dozens of volunteers throughout Florida spend their days working at wildlife sanctuaries, helping to rehabilitate pelicans that are found wrapped in monofilament line or pierced with fishhooks. Working as part of a rescue and rehabilitation team may be fascinating and rewarding; still, by holding out for opportunities of this type, one may miss other chances to contribute.

The following pages examine a handful of wildlife species that have become imperiled as a result of human activity. Some of these animals are coastal; others come to the shore to lay their eggs. Some are pelagic, keeping to the open ocean, but become stranded along the coast for reasons not fully understood. These animals in no way represent the vast diversity of species found along the Coastal United States. What they illustrate is the wide range of ways in which citizens can become involved in the conservation of coastal and marine wildlife.

MANATEES

"Sewer Sam"

When famed marine biologist Jacques Cousteau produced a TV documentary about manatees in the early 1970s, the film referred to these mammals as "shadowy, elusive creatures," "unloved," "neglected and ignored." Since then, thanks in part to Cousteau's moving portrayal, the public has come a long way toward understanding and appreciating these animals. But if manatees are to survive into the next century and beyond, the public must play a critical role in their conservation.

Cousteau's documentary told the story of a twelve-hundred-pound male manatee that had wandered into a thirty-three-inch-wide sewer line (attracted, presumably, by the fresh water). Sewer Sam, as this animal came to be called, was rescued from a Miami, Florida, storm drain and taken to nearby Miami Seaquarium for rehabilitation. There, in an isolated thirty-foot cement pool, Sam was destined to live the remainder of his life.

In a dramatic experiment that unfolded in the living rooms of thousands of viewers, Cousteau and his team maneuvered Sewer Sam into a large shipping crate and transported him six hundred miles to the Crystal River, a well-known wintering site for wild manatees. There, Sam was released into a remote but confined section of the river and observed by Cousteau's divers. Sam seemed to fare just fine in his new environment, and soon learned to dine on water hyacinths, which would become a staple in his new diet. After two weeks, the gates confining him were removed, and Sam was set free. Unfortunately, he had grown so accustomed to Cousteau's divers and so comfortable in his secluded enclave that the men had to harass him, splashing and yelling, to induce him to leave.

Finally, with a sonar transmitter attached to his tail, Sam meandered toward open waters. Within days, he had come across a small group of wild manatees that appeared to accept him. One of the last shots of Sam showed a huge, bewhiskered gray nose emerging from the water for air, and then disappearing.

Although the odyssey of Sewer Sam helped to rescue the manatee from obscurity, pressures facing these animals have only intensified in recent decades, and today there are fewer than twenty-five hundred of these endearing, seal-shaped herbivores remaining in the United States. The underlying reason is fairly simple: Manatees, more than any other species of marine mammal, are forced to share their habitat—the warm, shallow rivers, canals, and coastal waters of Florida and southern Georgia—with humans.

Being naturally slow-moving mammals that surface frequently for air, manatees are frequent victims of boat strikes. In fact, fully one-quarter of manatee mortalities each year can be traced to collisions with boats and barges: Either the manatee is fatally wounded by the propeller, or it is killed by the impact alone. The vast majority of living manatees, in fact, bear scars attesting to boat collisions they have endured in the past.

Speed on the part of recreational boaters is the primary cause of these collisions. Boaters racing through shallow waters are simply unable to see an animal lying beneath the water's surface in time to avoid hitting it. Manatees, which generally travel at top speeds of three to four miles an hour, have even less of a chance to move out of the way. Not surprisingly, animals hit by boats moving at full throttle are most likely to sustain serious or fatal injuries.

But boat collisions are just part of the problem. "Even if we were perfectly successful at stopping boat strikes," says biologist Pat Rose of Florida's Department of Environmental Protection, "unless we protect the manatee's habitat, the population is doomed."

With coastal development in Florida moving forward at an unprecedented pace (it is estimated that the state's population grows by some eight hundred new people each day), rivers and coastal regions that have traditionally served as feeding, resting, breeding, calving, and nursing grounds for manatees are under continual assault. Waters polluted by pesticides, fertilizer, human sewage, and urban runoff, and waters muddied by runoff from construction projects or the whirring blades of outboard motors, are not only less hospitable to manatees, but can no longer support the vital populations of sea grass and other greenery on which these mammals feed. (Consider, too, that a single adult manatee consumes as much as one hundred pounds of vegetation per day.)

Other problems arise as a result of the animals' close proximity to humans. Every year, manatees are crushed or drowned in canal locks and floodgates; and increasing numbers of manatees are stillborn, or die as infants, for reasons not yet fully understood. Debris takes its toll as well. Fishing line, nets, and crab traps get wrapped around manatees' flippers. Plastic bags, six-pack rings, and fishing gear are inadvertently ingested by the animals as they graze. Fishing hooks have been found embedded in manatees' lips, stuck in their tails, even lodged in their digestive tracts.

Getting Involved in Manatee Conservation

But even as the close association of humans and manatees threatens the survival of these animals, it also presents a tremendous opportunity for those who want to work on behalf of manatee conservation. The incidence of boat strikes, for example, can easily be reduced through public campaigns to educate boaters about the dangers of high speeds and to institute speed regulations where none exist. Anyone living near coastal waters inhabited by manatees should keep abreast of local planning issues and pay particular attention to the way coastal developments might affect adjacent waters. "It's important for people to remember," says Pat Rose, "that while land may be privately owned, the waters are a public resource. People need to speak up to protect them."

If steps are taken to protect the manatee, Rose points out, there will inevitably be many "spin-off" effects: Protecting the manatee means fighting for cleaner waters, which benefits untold numbers of plant and animal species. Protecting the manatee also means preserving underwater vegetation, which provides vital nursery grounds for fish and other marine animals. The manatee, in other words, is something of a flagship species that draws attention to the plight of the marine environment. "Ultimately," says Rose, "whether or not we are successful in protecting the manatee will likely decide whether a number of other species live or perish."

Finally, anyone interested in protecting the manatee is encouraged to support an organization with the expertise to fight for manatee conservation on many fronts. The highly regarded Save the Manatee Club runs an "Adopt-A-Manatee" program that funds research, education, rescue and rehabilitation, even lobbying efforts on behalf of these animals.

SEA TURTLES

"A Lone Loggerhead"
At about one in the morning, Louie Pierson, director of the Amber Lake Wildlife Refuge in Englewood, Florida, received a phone call from someone who had come across a turtle "coughing" on the beach. "It was a horrible, gagging-like noise," recalls Pierson, who arrived at the site about an hour later to see whether anything could be done for the animal.

The turtle, a loggerhead that weighed some 350 pounds, appeared to be choking on a twisted piece of black plastic sheeting. Pierson, with the help of several others who had congregated around the turtle, turned the animal onto its back and wedged its mouth open using a six-by-six-inch piece of pressure-treated lumber that he found lying nearby. "About two and a half feet of plastic was sticking out of the animal's mouth, but it was so slimy that I couldn't get a good hold on it, so I lay down next to the turtle and twisted the plastic around my arm."

He kept twisting, his hand moving farther down the throat of the turtle, until he felt he had a good grip. "I pulled, there was a huge sucking sound, and the rest of the plastic finally came out. The stench was so bad that I ran down to the water and dove in to rinse myself off. And the turtle, as soon as that plastic was out, bit down and crunched the lumber like it was balsa wood."

The plastic, it turned out, was a piece of sheeting measuring about eight by ten feet. Pierson believes the only reason more of the plastic was not ingested was that it had become snagged on a barnacle on the turtle's shell.

About an hour after the plastic was removed, the turtle was carried down to the edge of the water. From there, it disappeared into the waves.

Sadly, the ingestion of debris by sea turtles—notoriously indiscriminate eaters—is anything but uncommon. Scientists, examining the mouths, esophagi, and stomachs of living and dead sea turtles, have discovered startling quantities of debris, with bits of tar (from boat bilges), plastic resin pellets, chunks of plastic objects, balloons, monofilament line, and fishing hooks leading the list of ingested items. According to the Center for Marine Conservation, a juvenile hawksbill turtle found on a beach in Hawaii was discovered to have ingested an eight-inch-square plastic bag, a golf tee, chunks of plastic bag and sheeting, pieces of monofilament line, a plastic flower, part of a bottle cap, a comb, chips of Styrofoam, and dozens of small, round plastic pieces. The animal weighed eleven pounds, two of which were nothing but plastic.

And the debris is not just ingested. Routinely, sea turtles become entangled in fishing nets, fishing lines, and "onion sacks" (mesh bags used to store vegetables aboard ships). And as Carole Allen, founder and director of a conservation organization called HEART (Help Endangered Animals—Ridley Turtles) points out, debris can even interfere with nesting. "I've seen sections of the Texas coast that were so thick with debris," says Allen, "that if a turtle wanted to come ashore to lay her eggs, she quite literally could not make her way up the beach to dig a nest."

For nesting turtles, however, coastal development, and not debris, poses the greatest threat. In coastal regions of the southeastern United States, development often means the construction of seawalls and stone revetments, designed to protect near-shore buildings from the forces of erosion and heavy tides. David Godfrey, director of the Sea Turtle Survival League, points out that coastal armoring of this type destroys the dynamic, ever-shifting landscape of the coast. Sand is locked behind the revetment, erosion is increased on the beach below, and the landscape is rendered totally inhospitable to nesting turtles. "A female turtle," says Godfrey, "unable to find a suitable nesting site, may deposit her eggs in the water, where they will die. If she does lay her eggs on what little beach remains, the eggs are likely to be uncovered and washed away with the next high tide." According to Godfrey, close to one-third of Florida's beaches have already been shored up with revetments of some type.

Another threat associated with development is beachfront lighting. Female turtles tend not to come ashore to lay their eggs on lit beaches. But if hatchlings emerge from their nest onto a lit beach, they will become disoriented and head in the direction of the lights—and toward certain death—rather than crawl toward the water as they should.

Perhaps the most controversial threat to sea turtles comes in the form of shrimpers' nets. When these huge nets, or trawls, sweep through the water, they pick up everything in their path—shrimp, fish, crabs, jellyfish, debris, and sea turtles. Each year thousands of sea turtles needlessly drown in these nets: In 1994 alone, more than twenty-one hundred turtles are believed to have been killed this way. In the southeastern United States, shrimp boats are required by federal regulation to install in their nets devices called TEDs (turtle excluder devices), which provide a trapdoor of sorts through which turtles can escape. And indeed, many shrimpers willingly use TEDs, and use them properly. But overwhelming evidence, which correlates open shrimping season with the incidence of dead turtles that wash ashore, suggests that large numbers of sea turtles continue to drown in shrimp trawls. If further restrictions were placed on the types of TEDs used, and if shrimping were reduced in areas where turtles are found in abundance, these drownings might well decline.

Getting Involved in Sea Turtle Conservation

Of the world's eight species of sea turtles—all of which are considered threatened or endangered—five species nest along the Coastal United States. It is here, in these coastal regions, that volunteers can play a vital role in sea turtle conservation: first by gathering information about these animals, but also by helping to educate the public about the need to protect the turtles. Volunteers with the Sea Turtle Stranding Network, which is run by the National Marine Fisheries Service, are responsible for obtaining data from stranded turtles—that is, those that have washed ashore. If a stranded turtle is injured or entangled, the volunteer makes sure it is taken to an appropriate rehabilitation facility. If the animal is dead (which is the case in the vast majority of turtle strandings), the volunteer weighs, measures, and, occasionally, necropsies the animal, then disposes of the carcass. Although work of this type is neither glamorous nor uplifting, it is enormously valuable, for the information yielded by stranded turtles is channeled to state and federal agencies, which in turn use it to make legislative decisions regarding sea turtle conservation.

Important data is also gathered by turtle patrol organizations, which focus not on dead turtles, but rather on turtle nests. One of many such patrol groups is called Turtle Time, Inc.; located in Ft. Myers Beach, Florida it is some sixty members strong. At the break of dawn each day, Turtle Time volunteers walk the beaches in search of turtle tracks. When nests are found at the end of these tracks, they are monitored; and later, after any hatchlings have emerged, they are excavated so that information can be gathered on the apparent number of eggs, the number of successful hatchings, and so on.

Turtle Time volunteers also do everything in their power to ensure that hatchlings have an optimal chance of making it out of the nest and down to the water alive—by marking off nest sites so that the general public will not disturb them, patrolling the beach at night to check for dangerous beachfront lighting, and "blitzing the community," in the words of director Eve Haverfield, to educate residents and visitors about how to make the beaches more "turtle-friendly" during nesting season (May 1 through October 31). Realty agencies, for example, are provided with brochures to leave in rental cottages, as well as stickers to be placed above light switches, reminding visitors to keep lights off during nesting season. In Haverfield's view, the volunteers' efforts are paying off. In 1989, when the organization was just getting under way, only five viable nests could be found. During the 1995 nesting season, Haverfield and her colleagues counted forty-six.

The Sea Turtle Survival League has taken a different approach to turtle conservation, and, with membership support, has put its energies into establishing a national sea turtle refuge along the eastern coast of Florida. But League director David Godfrey, acknowledging that much of Florida's coast is already highly developed, urges individuals in coastal communities to push for local ordinances that restrict near-beach lighting and seawall construction. "The shores of Florida provide about 90 percent of all nesting habitat for sea turtles in the United States," says Godfrey, "and whatever is done to protect or destroy these shorelines is going to have a significant impact on turtle populations."

One of the toughest issues for the public to address is the drowning of turtles in nets. The Turtle Restoration Project, carried out by the Earth Island Institute in San Francisco, California, has tackled this problem by creating the "turtle-safe shrimp" campaign. According to Todd Steiner, campaign director, shrimpers whose catch carries the "turtle-safe" logo have agreed to use turtle excluder devices and to allow inspectors to monitor their boats. "There are many shrimpers who use TEDs because these devices enable them to pick up less by-catch, which improves the quality of their shrimp," says Steiner. "The goal of the campaign is to promote those shrimpers who are doing the right thing."

Steiner envisions a day when "turtle-safe shrimp" will carry the same clout as "dolphin-safe tuna." In the meantime, he encourages consumers, and travelers in particular, to use their purchasing power in other ways to help turtles. Tortoiseshell products sold in the Caribbean, for example, are often made from the shells of endangered sea turtles. These, as well as boots, shoes, and purses made from turtle leather, should be avoided.

WHALES AND OTHER MARINE MAMMALS

"Nicholas" and "Alexander"
In August 1989, The Marine Mammal Center (TMMC) in Sausalito, California, received word of two beached dolphins on San Francisco's Ocean Beach. When the rescue team arrived at the scene of the stranding, members could see almost immediately that these were not dolphins: Despite their large, rounded heads and long snouts, the gray-brown mammals

appeared instead to be a species of rarely seen, deep-sea cetaceans known as beaked whales.

Whales and dolphins "strand," or come ashore, for a variety of reasons that are not well understood. Researchers speculate that in some instances, when an animal is injured or extremely sick, it will come ashore as a desperate alternative to drowning. When this happens, the animal is usually beyond the help of any rescue team. The two whales on Ocean Beach, however, did not appear to be quite so critical. Under the gaze of hundreds of onlookers, the animals were stabilized, their respiration noted, and their blood drawn for an analysis of their condition. Eventually, the two were loaded onto a flatbed truck and tranported forty miles to Marine World in Vallejo.

There, in round-the-clock, four-hour shifts, volunteers kept an eye on the whales' respiration and movements, while TMMC's animal-care team tried to determine what might have caused them to strand. The two were named Nicholas and Alexander.

From the start, Nicholas and Alexander were big news, for no one had ever before attempted to rescue and rehabilitate any species of beaked whale. When the animals surprised many by surviving their first night, as well as the next and the next, "Get Whale" cards and letters began arriving in the mail, and a local newspaper started providing daily updates on the whales' condition. One expert on beaked whales, upon learning of the rescue, cut short a trip to Italy and headed for California.

The beaked whale specialist, upon arrival, identified the two animals as Cuvier's beaked whales. But perhaps more importantly, he confirmed what the animal-care team had already conjectured: that these two mammals, six to eight hundred pounds apiece, were in fact newborns.

Normally, whales of this age would survive solely on their mothers' milk, which is rich in immune system components. As a substitute for these natural defenses, TMMC staff administered a form of gamma globulin that had been specially prepared for the whales at the University of California, Berkeley. Feeding represented something of a challenge, for although both whales seemed to enjoy sucking on the fingers of their human caregivers, neither would take a bottle. Finally, each infant was encouraged to take formula from a nipple placed next to a human finger. The nipple was attached to a long IV tube, which was connected to a large formula-filled syringe. The formula consisted of ground smelt and herring, mixed with commercial milk formula, peanut oil, lecithin, and vitamins. Eventually, both whales learned to suckle from a nipple attached to a baby bottle.

Nicholas and Alexander seemed to respond well to the care they received, and grew more active as the days progressed. Blood tests in each animal, however, revealed that an infection was developing despite treatment. Sixteen days after his rescue, Nicholas suddenly stopped swimming and sank to the bottom of the tank. Mouth-to-blowhole resuscitation was attempted, but with no luck. Nine days later Alexander died as well. Both, it turned out, had been suffering from pneumonia.

Tissue samples from the whales were sent to researchers throughout the country. It was the samples tested by the Environmental Protection Agency, however, that proved to be most enlightening: Tissues from both Nicholas and Alexander contained high levels of PCBs (polychlorinated biphenyls) and DDE, a form of the pesticide DDT. Since both whales became ill long before they were weaned, scientists believe the animals must have ingested the contaminants through their mothers' milk.

"Inky"

On Thanksgiving night in 1993, a young female pygmy sperm whale, weighing just over two hundred pounds, was found stranded off the New Jersey coast. After spending a night at the Marine Mammal Stranding Center in Brigantine, New Jersey, she was flown in a Coast Guard helicopter to Baltimore and transported to the National Aquarium.

The whale's first medical assessment showed her to be in critical condition. During the next few weeks, she was treated for dehydration, respiratory infection, gastrointestinal distress, and parasitic and fungal infections. She was also given physical therapy, since some of her muscles had atrophied as a result of the stranding. And from the minute she arrived, she was put under a twenty-four-hour watch by a team of trained volunteers from the Marine Animal Rescue Team. Because of the ink-like substance that she and other members of her species release into the water, her caretakers named her Inky.

Despite the top-flight medical attention she received, Inky continued to exhibit some serious problems well into December. David Schofield, chief mammalogist and coordinator of the aquarium's Marine Animal Rescue Program, says that several things continued to trouble her caretakers. "We had expected her to eat about twenty-two pounds of fish a day, but after eating about half of that, she would start throwing up. In addition, she was doing a tremendous amount of arching, flexing her tail and head inward, as if she had painful abdominal cramping." The team also noticed that she was unable to dive: At every attempt, she would bob back up to the surface like a cork.

In an attempt to discover what was at the root of Inky's problems, Schofield and his colleagues finally decided to perform an endoscopy. "We went in looking for a gastrointestinal problem," says Schofield, "and what we found was lots of plastic." For the next six weeks, through a series of six procedures, the medical team located and removed pieces of Mylar balloons, clear plastic bags, and garbage bags.

There are a number of ways Inky could have ingested the debris: Lunging at a squid, for example, she may have inadvertently gotten a mouthful of floating garbage. And because she was young and recently weaned, it is conceivable that she was unable to differentiate between edible and inedible materials. The bottom line, however, is that debris was abundant in the waters she inhabited.

As more and more debris was removed, Inky's condition improved. By the following May she had grown more than a foot and had gained 125 pounds. She learned to play with toys in the pool, and was able to chase and catch live fish. At the end of May, Inky was transported via navy cargo plane to Florida, fitted with a radio transmitter, and released thirty miles offshore. By all accounts, she was healthy and well equipped to survive.

There is no way of knowing how many thousands of marine mammals are killed each year from ingesting or becoming entangled in debris, or from living in an environment laced with toxins.

Oceanborne contaminants are particularly insidious, not only because they are invisible, but also because, quite simply, they do not break down. Instead, substances such as PCBs and DDT reside in the tissues of plants and animals, accumulating in greater and greater concentrations as they are passed up the food chain, or as they are passed from mother to offspring.

The well-known whale biologist Roger Payne, of the Whale Conservation Institute, has been particularly effective in bringing the contaminant problem into perspective for the general public. To illustrate the extent of toxic contamination in the marine environment, Payne points out that food with more than 5 parts per million of PCBs, according to the U.S. government, is unfit for human consumption. If something contains more than 50 parts per million of PCBs, moreover, it must be transported in specially marked containers and incinerated at a specific temperature. Whales and other predators that exist at the top of what Payne refers to as the "oceanic food pyramid" are not subject to such regulations, but if they were, those that are most contaminated might be classified—to quote Payne—as "swimming toxic dump sites." Tissue samples from killer whales living far from shore were found to contain PCB concentrations of 400 parts per million. Beluga whales living in an estuary on Canada's St. Lawrence River—a population suffering from a high incidence of tumors, developmental abnormalities, and below-average birthrates—averaged PCB concentrations of 600 parts per million.

The precise role of these contaminants in the deaths of animals like Nicholas and Alexander, or in the increasing number of marine mammal die-offs (since 1978, at least twelve such die-offs have been reported), has yet to be established. Unlike debris that becomes wrapped around an animal's flipper, incapacitating the animal or causing a deadly infection, a contaminant cannot so easily be indicted in an animal's death. Nonetheless, scientists have shown that some of these contaminants, PCBs included, can compromise an animal's immune system, rendering that animal susceptible to diseases such as pneumonia and cancer.

Incidentally, PCBs, DDT, and other so-called chemical contaminants are just part of the problem. Biological contaminants—bacteria, viruses, and nutrients that are transmitted to coastal waters through sewage waste (see chapter 2, "Campaigning for Cleaner Waters")—may also be quite dangerous. When excessive amounts of nutrients, for example, enter coastal waters under certain environmental conditions, they can spur the explosive growth of red or brown algae, which produce a particular type of toxin that is deadly to marine mammals.

Getting Involved in Marine Mammal Conservation
Fortunately, there are many highly regarded organizations that work on behalf of marine mammals—carrying out research, educating the public, performing rescue and rehabilitation services, and working for the passage of legislation (including provisions for cleaner water)—to help ensure the continued survival of these species. It is vital that these organizations be supported, both through the efforts of volunteers and through membership contributions.

There are also a handful of ways in which the public can work a bit more closely with marine mammals. Under the direction of the National Marine Fisheries Service, there are five regional Marine Mammal Stranding Networks whose volunteers respond to virtually all reported strandings. Stranding volunteers, many of whom are trained in animal handling or a related field, evaluate the animal in question and help to decide whether it should be returned to sea, taken to a facility for rehabilitation, or euthanized. Because dead animals can provide a wealth of information about the biology, pathology, and mortality of their species, certain stranding volunteers are also responsible for performing marine mammal postmortems.

"Volunteers are very important to the stranding network," says Greg Early, stranding coordinator for the New England Aquarium, "but people should realize that it is very important for them to work within the existing network structure. It is illegal and dangerous to approach a marine animal unsupervised, and you are guaranteed to do the animal more harm than good." Anyone who comes across what appears to be a stranded marine mammal should not simply take matters into his or her own hands; instead, he or she should observe the animal and report it to the stranding network.

"People need to understand," says Early, "that being a competent pair of eyes and ears is a vital role." If someone wants to get in touch with a local network with information about a stranded animal, Early suggests contacting a local law enforcement agency.

Although some marine mammal facilities rely on paid staff for the care and rehabilitation of these animals, others combine the expertise of staff and volunteers. At The Marine

Mammal Center in Sausalito, California, 95 percent of the staff are volunteers. These volunteers (who are referred to, incidentally, as "staff") help care for anywhere from five hundred to eight hundred injured, diseased, and orphaned seals, sea lions, cetaceans, and sea otters that come through The Center's doors each year. Volunteers take on many routine feeding duties (which may involve anything from tube-feeding newborn animals to dragging dead fish around a shallow tub to teach young seals to catch prey), perform lab tests, and carry out rescues and releases. Many of the animals under rehabilitation suffer from problems related to human impact: Patients include harbor seal pups born with suppressed immune systems, sea otters drenched in oil, elephant seals suffering from skin disease, sea lions wounded (often fatally) from gunshots, and an assortment of animals desperately entangled in gill nets and other debris.

Rescue and rehabilitation facilities such as TMMC provide an exciting opportunity for volunteers who are impassioned about marine mammals and dedicated to the idea that these animals deserve some sort of second chance to survive alongside humans.

THE PIPING PLOVER AND THE COMPETITION FOR COAST

Although the tiny, sand-colored shorebirds called piping plovers have been protected under the Endangered Species Act since 1986, only a small fraction of their nesting habitat has been set aside for conservation purposes. The future of these remarkably inconspicuous birds—still recovering after having been hunted to near extinction early in this century—hinges on what happens along the stretches of beach that they currently share with humans.

Because of their nesting and behavior patterns, plovers are unusually vulnerable to human disturbance. Their nests, for example, which are no more than small depressions in the sand, are located along flat, exposed stretches of beach between the high-water mark and the foot of the dunes. Plovers are not bold birds: Unlike terns, which nest in colonies and are notorious for dive-bombing anything that wanders into their territory, adult plovers respond to threats by feigning injury, thereby distracting the intruder from the nest, or by abandoning the nest altogether.

Plover chicks, for the first few hours after hatching, evade predators simply by remaining motionless. Once they are mobile, however, they expose themselves to the perils of the beach by foraging alongside their parents, combing through the washed-up strip of seaweed known as the tidal wrack in search of sand flies, or locating tiny invertebrates living in the sands of the tidal pools.

Coastal development has all kinds of potentially harmful implications for these tiny birds. Even armoring a section of coastline can cause problems. A simple jetty, for example, acts as a barrier to foraging chicks, which require up to a mile of shoreline to find adequate supplies of food. And as more people take up residence in a coastal area, more garbage is produced, which often leads to a proliferation of landfills. The landfills, in turn, support unnaturally large populations of great black-backed and herring gulls, which easily displace the tiny plovers from their nesting areas.

The broad, flat expanses of clean beach that attract nesting plovers, moreover, are precisely the type of beach most preferred by human visitors. And because the nests and their inhabitants blend so beautifully into their surroundings, a visitor may arrive at the beach, throw down a beach towel, and settle in for the day, never realizing that he is only fifteen feet from a nest. In fact, plover nests can be so well camouflaged that they remain entirely undetected until they are stepped on. Another threat to plovers comes from the dogs that accompany their owners to the beach. Unlike people, dogs have no trouble locating plover families and can make a quick meal of either chicks or adults.

Damage caused by beachgoers on foot, however, pales in comparison to the devastation wreaked by off-road vehicles, or ORVs, which are given free rein on many of the barrier beaches along the Atlantic coast. For nesting plovers, the impact of ORVs is nothing short of catastrophic. As the vehicles travel along the beach, one after another, they create ruts that are too deep for the chicks to cross. They plow through the tidal wrack, grinding it into the sand, and run through the tidal pools, killing the tiny invertebrates that live just under the surface of the sand. And, as one might expect, they crush the plovers—eggs, chicks, and adults. On a stretch of shoreline sporting some five hundred ORVs—as many do—the birds hardly stand a chance.

Protecting the Plover

Today, on forty-five public beaches along Cape Cod, Martha's Vineyard, Nantucket, and Massachusetts's South Shore, piping plovers are benefiting from a grassroots conservation program run by the Massachusetts Audubon Society. From the first of April until the end of August, volunteers and interns fan out over these beaches to monitor the activities of plovers, terns, and other rare coastal waterbirds. When nests are found, signs alerting the public to their presence are posted, and protective fencing is erected. When a nest with plover chicks is found, program staff and volunteers close two hundred yards of beachfront to ORVs. (In places where this controversial step has been taken, plover populations have doubled annually.)

And at every opportunity, the volunteers try to educate beach visitors—by describing the birds and their habits, explaining the need to protect them, and sometimes showing the visitors a nest through a spotting scope.

"Our volunteers are for the most part local people," says Scott Hecker, director of the Coastal Waterbird Program. "They care about the beach; they know the people who come here. And beachgoers are more likely to listen to them than to some stranger from out of town. The bottom line is that, yes, we want beachgoers to obey the rules. But beyond that, we hope that they will also become aware of the birds, enjoy them, and conclude that they are worth protecting."

In Massachusetts, piping plovers are making a stronger comeback than in any other state. In 1986, officials counted about 125 plover pairs. Today, more than 450 pairs have been identified.

For anyone interested in helping the piping plover, Hecker offers these suggestions. First, respect signs that designate nesting areas, and avoid disturbing the birds. Keep dogs leashed. To become active in plover conservation, learn a bit about the birds and their habits (information is available from the Massachusetts Audubon Society, from other Audubon chapters, or from similar conservation organizations). Volunteer with a local wildlife-protection organization, or make a financial contribution. Remember, too, the ripple effect produced from plover conservation: More than a dozen coastal bird species, from black skimmers to American oystercatchers to horned larks, also feed along the tidal wracks, forage throughout estuaries, and require clean, quiet beaches for nesting. When the plover is protected, all of these birds benefit.

CALIFORNIA SEA OTTERS

Off the California coast lies a fantastically rich ecosystem known as the kelp forest. Here can be found octopi, eels, minnows, sharks, rays, and dozens of other marine species, all finding food and shelter amongst the vegetation and benefiting from the nutrients released by the kelp itself. The single enemy of the kelp forest is a spiny invertebrate known as the sea urchin. If left unchecked, sea urchins can devour the seaweed, replacing a teeming habitat with bare patches of rock or sand.

Sea otters, which dine on sea urchins, are quite literally the guardians of the kelp forest. Without these marine mammals, large swaths of the California kelp forests could disappear.

As many as twenty thousand southern sea otters once flourished along the California coast, their habitat stretching from the Baja peninsula to the Oregon border. Sadly, however, the animals proved irresistible to fur hunters, and by the beginning of the twentieth century only a handful remained.

Even today, California's sea otter population is a shadow of what it once was. Although protected under both the Marine Mammal Protection Act and the Endangered Species Act, southern sea otters, unlike their cousins living off the coasts of Alaska and Russia, have not rebounded. For reasons not fully understood, the population maintains a growth rate that is feeble in comparison with that of other otter subspecies.

Because southern sea otters number only about twenty-four hundred and inhabit a mere 250-mile stretch of coastline, these animals live under the continual threat of an oil spill off the California coast.

Sea otters are particularly susceptible to oil spills. Unlike marine mammals whose warmth derives from a thick layer of fat, otters rely on a dense undercoat whose hairs (some seventy of them per hair follicle) are designed to interlock with one another, creating tiny spaces in which insulating air bubbles are held. When an otter's coat becomes saturated with oil, the undercoat becomes slicked down, losing its ability to protect the animal. In less than an hour, a heavily oiled otter will become hypothermic and die.

Some oiled otters manage to clean their fur after a spill—only to become poisoned from ingesting oil during the grooming process. And even those otters lucky enough to escape any direct contact with the oil may succumb months after a spill, victims of oilborne toxins that have accumulated in the tissues of the clams, mussels, abalones, and sea urchins that make up the otters' diet.

In light of the fact that the 1989 Exxon *Valdez* spill killed upwards of thirty-five hundred sea otters, it is quite conceivable that a similar spill off the California coast would completely wipe out the existing population of southern sea otters.

Fortunately, under the direction of the U.S. Coast Guard and the State Office of Oil Spill Prevention and Response (OSPR), a contingency plan has been developed so that in the event of such a catastrophe, the coastal environment can be cleaned up as rapidly as possible and some of its natural resources—including sea otters—saved. To facilitate an emergency response of this type, the California Ocean Assistance Spill Team, or COAST, has been developed.

The purpose of COAST is to recruit volunteers for the myriad tasks that will need to be carried out in the wake of an oil spill. Some 250 volunteers have already signed up with the program, and stand ready to move into their designated jobs at a moment's notice. Some will drive trucks, others will direct traffic. Some will run errands for those working at a command center, while others will transport supplies to those carrying out the coastline cleanup. Some of the duties are reserved for those with special training. Volunteers who are skilled in animal rescue and rehabilitation, for example, will take on the washing and drying of otters and other oiled animals.

COAST is the brainchild of an organization called Friends of the Sea Otter (FSO), a Monterey-based advocacy group. Since its inception in 1968, FSO has proven to be a formidable force in sea otter conservation, educating citizens throughout the country about sea otters and providing them with the tools to fight for the otters' protection. "When an important issue comes up on the national agenda that will impact sea otters," says Ellen Faurot-Daniels, FSO science director, "we ask our members to cast their vote, so to speak, with their elected official, letting them know how they'd like that official to vote."

In 1977, FSO members were instrumental in persuading legislators to grant the southern sea otter "threatened" status under the Endangered Species Act. In the mid-1980s, after researchers learned that eighty to one hundred otters were drowning each year in gill nets, members mobilized again, and through a massive campaign launched through letters and phone calls, convinced state legislators to enact a law on the otters' behalf. Today, gill nets have been restricted to waters of a certain depth, and the incidental drowning of otters has largely been eliminated.

Beyond working for the conservation of the species as a whole, there are those who have taken on the task of saving these animals one by one. At the Monterey Bay Aquarium's Sea Otter Research and Conservation Program, staff and volunteers dedicate their days and nights to rehabilitating otters that are sick, injured, or orphaned.

The program for orphaned otters is particularly intensive. As soon as these animals are brought into the aquarium (some as young as a day old), they are assigned human surrogates who feed, groom, and nurture them around the clock. As soon as these surrogate "moms" are confident that their pups have bonded to them, they begin taking them to shallow tidal pools, encouraging the young otters to explore their surroundings and helping them locate food. Later, the young otters are taken on "swims" in the open ocean, where their "moms" demonstrate skills such as diving for shellfish. As the otters gain confidence and independence, they stay out longer and longer on these expeditions. The day a young otter decides not to follow its "mom" back to the aquarium is the day of its release.

Even after the otters have made the transition back to the wild, aquarium staff and volunteers try to keep the animals under close watch, and, if necessary, intervene on the otters' behalf. Some of these animals survive in the wild, others do not.*

The situation of the southern sea otter, given its low numbers and geographically limited range, could still be considered somewhat precarious. And yet, because these animals are so charismatic, they have attracted quite a bit of attention and support. Susan Brown, executive director of Friends of the Sea Otter, points out that this places an even greater responsibility on humans to protect them. "These animals are instrumental to the kelp forest ecosystem," says Brown. "They are a very visible indicator of the health of their environment. And they have become important to our economy: People come to Monterey just to see them. But beyond that, otters are some of the most engaging marine mammals in existence, and when you see one, you are totally smitten. In my opinion, if we can't manage to protect the sea otter—an animal with all these things in its favor—then what can we protect?"

A FINAL SUGGESTION

Beyond working on behalf of individual species, consider two actions whose benefits extend to marine and coastal creatures of all kinds.

First, make your views on coastal issues known to federal and state legislators. Write in support of endangered species, in support of clean water, in support of policies that protect coastal habitat. "Individuals are engaged in environmental battles at every level—by cleaning their beaches of plastic, by working for the protection of species habitat, by buying recycled products, and in plenty of other ways," says David Godfrey of the Sea Turtle Survival League. "These battles are very important, and they're necessary. But if we allow legislators to weaken the laws that are protecting the wildlife, we're going to lose the war."

The importance of the public's voice should not be underestimated. Decades ago, when citizens and the scientific community became concerned about the clubbing of baby harp seals, the decimation of the whale species through commercial hunting, and the annual deaths of half a million dolphins in tuna nets, they responded with public outcry. Congress, in turn, passed the Marine Mammal Protection Act, a historic piece of legislation that, with certain exceptions, forbids the taking of any marine mammal in U.S. waters.

Individuals also need to keep in mind that, as exciting as it may be to help rescue an entangled seal, it is every bit as important to curb debris before it takes its toll on marine and coastal wildlife. The bulk of marine debris comes not from the likes of fishing boats, cruise ships, merchant shippers, and recreational boaters; a shocking 70 to 80 percent of it (with a few, localized exceptions) stems from *land-based sources*. The sandwich bag that ends up choking a turtle, in other words, might have once blown out the window of a truck into a field miles from the coast. Eventually it washed into a creek, was carried down to a river, and was transported to the ocean. If more people were to clean up after themselves, join in annual cleanups, and spread the word about the dangers of marine debris, coastal and marine environments would be far safer for wildlife.

FOR MORE INFORMATION

For general information on coastal and marine wildlife issues:

CENTER FOR MARINE CONSERVATION
1725 DeSales Street, NW
Washington, D.C. 20036
(202) 429-5609

WORLD WILDLIFE FUND
1250 24th Street, NW
Washington, D.C. 20037
(202) 293-4800

For information on manatee conservation:

FLORIDA POWER AND LIGHT COMPANY
Environmental Affairs
P.O. Box 088801
North Palm Beach, FL 33408-8801
(800) 552-8440

Produces an excellent booklet entitled "The West Indian Manatee in Florida."

SAVE THE MANATEE CLUB
500 North Maitland Avenue
Maitland, FL 32751
(800) 432-JOIN

Established in 1981 by singer Jimmy Buffett to promote public awareness and education about the manatee.

Informational brochures about manatees for boaters, divers, and others who might come across these animals may be obtained from:

BUREAU OF PROTECTED SPECIES
Florida Department of Environmental Protection
3900 Commonwealth Boulevard
Mail Station 245
Tallahassee, FL 32399

To report an injured, dead, harassed, tagged, or orphaned manatee, contact the Florida Marine Patrol at 1-800-DIAL-FMP.

For information on sea turtle conservation:

THE SEA TURTLE SURVIVAL LEAGUE
4424 N.W. 13th Street, Suite A-1
Gainesville, FL 32609
(800) 678-7853

Supports sea turtle research and conservation and works toward the establishment of the Archie Carr Wildlife Refuge. Is part of the Caribbean Conservation Corporation.

SEA TURTLE RESTORATION PROJECT
300 Broadway
San Francisco, CA 94133
(800) 859-SAVE

TURTLE TIME, INC.
P.O. Box 2621
Ft. Myers, FL 33932

To find out whether a turtle patrol organization exists in a particular community, residents of Florida can call the state's Department of Environmental Protection at (813) 896-8626.

SEA TURTLE STRANDING AND SALVAGE NETWORK
National Marine Fisheries Service
Miami Laboratory
75 Virginia Beach Drive
Miami, FL 33149
(305) 361-5761

CAROLE ALLEN
HEART
P.O. Box 681231
Houston, TX 77268-1231
(713) 444-6204

For information on marine mammal conservation:

THE MARINE MAMMAL CENTER
Marin Headlands
Golden Gate National Recreation Area
Sausalito, CA 94965
(415) 289-7325

THE NATIONAL AQUARIUM IN BALTIMORE
Marine Animal Rescue Program (MARP)
Pier 3
501 East Pratt Street
Baltimore, MD 21202-3194

THE CENTER FOR COASTAL STUDIES
59 Commercial Street
Box 1036
Provincetown, MA 02657
(508) 487-3622

In addition to whale research, the Center maintains a small, highly trained team for whale disentanglement.

WHALE CONSERVATION INSTITUTE
191 Weston Road
Lincoln, MA 01773
(617) 259-0423

THE MARINE MAMMAL COMMISSION
1825 Connecticut Avenue, NW #512
Washington, D.C. 20009
(202) 606-5504

There are five regional marine mammal stranding centers:

NATIONAL MARINE FISHERIES SERVICE
Alaska Region
P.O. Box 21668
Juneau, AK 99802-1668

NATIONAL MARINE FISHERIES SERVICE
Northwest Region
7600 Sand Point Way, N.E.
Seattle, WA 98115-0070

NATIONAL MARINE FISHERIES SERVICE
Southwest Region
501 West Ocean Boulevard
Suite 4200
Long Beach, CA 90802-4213

NATIONAL MARINE FISHERIES SERVICE
Southeast Region
9721 Executive Center Drive, North
St. Petersburg, FL 33702-2432

NATIONAL MARINE FISHERIES SERVICE
Northeast Region
One Blackburn Drive
Gloucester, MA 01930-2298

For information about the Massachusetts Audubon Society's Coastal Waterbird Program:

COASTAL WATERBIRD PROGRAM
Massachusetts Audubon Society
2000 Main Street
Marshfield, MA 02050
(617) 834-9661

For information about similar coastal waterbird programs on the West Coast:

NATIONAL AUDUBON SOCIETY
California State Field Office
555 Audubon Place
Sacramento, CA 95825
(916) 481-5332

For information about sea otter conservation:

FRIENDS OF THE SEA OTTER
2150 Garden Road, B-4
Monterey, CA 93940
(408) 373-2747

THE MONTEREY BAY AQUARIUM
Sea Otter Research and Conservation Program
886 Cannery Row
Monterey, CA 93940
(408) 648-4800

Two organizations that specialize in the rescue and rehabilitation of coastal birds, especially those that are caught in fishing equipment, are:

SUNCOAST SEABIRD SANCTUARY
18328 Gulf Boulevard
Indian Shore
St. Petersburg, FL 34635
(813) 391-6211

PELICAN MAN'S BIRD SANCTUARY
1708 Ken Thompson Parkway
Sarasota, FL 34236
(813) 388-4444

*In April 1996, the sea otter rehabilitation efforts described here were removed from the Monterey Bay Aquarium to The Marine Mammal Center in Sausalito, California. The aquarium continues to focus on research studies, involving both captive and wild otter populations, that will contribute to the long-term survival of these threatened animals.

What Citizens Can Do

Tempting as it may be to cling to the notion that our own daily actions have little or no ecological impact, what must be kept in mind is that these seemingly tiny acts, when added up, have a huge and in many areas devastating effect on our waters, both coastal and inland.

It is easy to comfort ourselves with the thought that the pesticides used to keep the insects off the roses, or the herbicides that keep the weeds out of the lawn, are applied in such negligibly small amounts that they hardly make a difference to groundwater or local streams. But as a group, homeowners purchase tens of millions of pounds of insecticides, herbicides, and fungicides each year to care for their own small patches of lawn and garden. And by some estimates, urban gardeners use as much as ten times the amount of toxic chemicals per acre as farmers.

Whether we are watering the lawn, scraping the hull of a boat, repairing the car engine, or even walking along the beach, we can make choices that will affect the quality of our waters.

FIRST OF ALL, WHY CONSERVE WATER?

There are many reasons to conserve water. When municipal sewage systems or septic tanks are burdened with excessive amounts of water, they work less effectively in cleaning the water that moves through them, which means that when water is discharged, it is likely to contain more pollutants. In cities with combined sewer overflows (CSOs), the situation is even worse: When CSOs become overwhelmed with too much water, sewage is diverted into the storm-drain system, which carries it straight to local waterways.

GARDENING AND LAWN CARE

Pest management
Toxins found in many common pesticides inevitably wind up in nearby streams, lakes, estuaries, and offshore waters, poisoning aquatic organisms and accumulating in greater and greater concentrations as they move up the food chain.

Instead of eradicating entire populations of garden pests, learn a bit about Integrated Pest Management (IPM), a method aimed at keeping harmful pest populations in check by relying on a variety of natural control techniques. IPM methods include pruning infested parts of a plant, washing off insects with water or insecticidal soap, hand-killing the pests, or introducing predators such as ladybugs or praying mantises.

Fertilization
Excessive applications of lawn and garden fertilizer can leach into nearby streams, lakes, and near-shore waters, loading them

with nutrients (primarily nitrogen and phosphorus) that create an oxygen-starved aquatic environment.

Consider using natural fertilizers, such as compost, manure, or commercially available organic products. These substances tend to be released slowly into the soil so that excess nutrients are not washed away.

Conserving Water

Sweep off the driveway, sidewalk, or terrace rather than hosing it down.

Avoid overwatering the lawn or garden. Excess water, which may contain residues from pesticides or fertilizers, will often flow onto the sidewalk or driveway, thus carrying it straight into the storm-drain system.

Set sprinklers in the early morning or evening to reduce the amount of water lost to evaporation.

Whenever possible, select plant varieties that are well suited to the region and that do not require excessive amounts of watering.

Consider drip hoses, which provide adequate water without the waste sometimes associated with sprinklers.

Preventing Erosion and Discouraging Runoff

Runoff can carry toxins, nutrients, and eroded soil into nearby waterways.

Encourage water to seep into the soil by planting bare areas with ground covers, trees, or shrubs.

When landscaping around the house, try to use permeable surfaces (wooden decks, interlocking paving stones, bricks laid in sand rather than mortar, crushed gravel, etc.).

Direct downspouts onto areas covered with vegetation, rather than toward impermeable surfaces, so that the rainwater can be absorbed into the ground.

DRIVING AND CAR CARE

Never dump motor oil, antifreeze, or any other automobile fluids into the gutter or down the drain. Take used motor oil to a local service station for recycling. (Incidentally, antifreeze is deadly not only to aquatic life, but to dogs and cats as well, which are attracted to its sweet taste and lick it off driveway surfaces.)

Maintain your vehicle to prevent it from leaking dangerous fluids.

Wash your car on the lawn or on another permeable surface. This way, the water can seep into the soil where it can be filtered; otherwise, it will wash into the storm-drain system. Use a low-phosphate detergent.

Drive less. Driving is a major source not only of air pollution, but of water pollution as well. Certain metals, for example, that are highly toxic to aquatic life are routinely deposited on roads by cars. As brake pads wear down, they emit copper. Automobile tires, as they wear down, deposit cadmium and zinc. Every time it rains, these metals, as well as oil, grease, and other toxic substances, are washed right off the surfaces of roads, highways, and parking lots and into the storm-drain system.

INSIDE THE HOUSE

Neither sewage-treatment plants nor septic systems are designed to clean water of toxins. These substances can pass right through either a treatment plant or a septic system, often killing the system's vital bacteria in the process, and end up in groundwater or in a nearby waterway.

Whenever possible, use cleaning products containing non-toxic substances. Some of these products are commercially available, and others can be made using substances such as vinegar, baking soda, and salt. (A quart of water mixed with one cup of vinegar, for example, makes a good window cleaner.)

Try to use low-phosphate or phosphate-free detergents.

Never assume that common household products can be safely poured down the drain or flushed down a toilet: Items such as paints, solvents, cleaners, and drain cleaners may contain potent toxins, and should be disposed of either in the garbage or at a hazardous-household-waste collection site. Read directions on all product containers and dispose of the products responsibly.

Conserve water by fixing leaky faucets and toilets. A single leaky tap can waste as much as twenty gallons of water a day.

Install a showerhead that uses less water.

Turn off the tap while shaving, brushing teeth, or washing dishes (as much as a gallon of water can flow from a faucet in sixty seconds).

Place a water-filled plastic jug (not a brick) in the toilet tank to reduce the amount of water used during each flush.

Wash only full loads in the washing machine or dishwasher.

Refrain from using the disposal under the kitchen sink. It requires lots of water and burdens the septic system or the local sewage plant with additional organic material. Instead, throw your kitchen scraps into the garbage can, or better yet, compost them.

WATCHING THE SEPTIC SYSTEM

Keeping septic systems well maintained and running smoothly ensures that impurities do not escape from the system and contaminate ground water.

Have the septic system cleaned every three to five years.

OUT FOR A STROLL

Pick up after your pet. Pet waste left on or near the street can be washed into the storm-drain system and carried into a local waterway, where it contributes not only organic matter but bacteria as well.

BEING AN ENVIRONMENTALLY RESPONSIBLE SHOPPER

Whenever possible, shop with your own supply of string or canvas bags.

Avoid buying products with excessive amounts of packaging—especially plastic packaging.

If you buy products that are packaged with six-pack rings, snip the rings before throwing them out.

Try to avoid products packaged in Styrofoam, which lasts for hundreds of years in the marine environment.

OUT ON THE BOAT

Never release raw sewage from a boat; instead, empty the

boat's bilge at an onshore pump-out facility.

Keep a covered garbage receptacle on board so that no debris gets blown overboard. Whenever possible, pick up debris found floating on the water.

When navigating a motorboat through waters near to shore or in protected coves or waterways, travel slowly to keep wake to a minimum: Large, powerful wake contributes to shoreline erosion. When a boat moves slowly through shallow waters, the engine is also less likely to tear up beds of sea grass and churn up bottom sediment.

Keep in mind that many of the paints and cleaning products for boat hulls are highly toxic to marine life. Even when the boat is taken out of the water for repair, be watchful of these products. Spread a drop cloth under the boat before chipping off old paint, and use low-phosphate detergent when cleaning the boat hull.

Recycle your boat's used motor oil.

Consider distributing information on environmentally responsible boating and fishing practices at your marina. Information is available from the Center for Marine Conservation.

If you are fishing, be sure to dispose of old hooks, monofilament fishing line, and other fishing equipment responsibly. If line becomes snarled, try to retrieve it rather than simply cutting and discarding it.

MAKING YOUR VIEWS KNOWN

By all means, write your senator or representative to express your views on environmental issues. Here are a few tips for writing an effective letter:

☀ *Type or neatly write the letter using a business-letter format.*

☀ *State your point clearly in the first paragraph ("I am writing in support of the Endangered Species Act," etc.), then go on to support your point in the next paragraph or two. Keep the letter short and to the point.*

☀ *Make sure to include a return address on the letter itself.*

Address the letter as follows:

> The Honorable [name] or Senator [name]
> U.S. Senate
> Washington, D.C. 20510

> The Honorable [name] or Representative [name]
> U.S. House of Representatives
> Washington, D.C. 20515

AND KEEP IN MIND . . .

For Beaches and Oceans that are Free of Debris

Cigarette butts are *not* biodegradable! Whether you are on the beach, in a boat, or at a bus stop, don't flick your cigarette butt. Put it out and throw it away.

Set aside a few hours on the third Saturday of each September and join the International Coastal Cleanup. For information on this and other cleanup-related activities, contact the Center for Marine Conservation.

Initiate a coastal or inland-waterway cleanup of your own.

If you are a diver, consider organizing an underwater cleanup with fellow divers.

Organize a storm-drain stenciling program in your community to spread the word that whatever flows into the storm-drain system will wind up, untreated, in the nearest waterway.

If you are decorating with balloons, make sure the balloons do not float away. Educate others about the dangers that balloons can pose to marine wildlife.

If you plan to embark on a cruise, learn about environmentally responsible cruise line practices. A cruise line information packet is available from the Center for Marine Conservation.

For Cleaner Water

Hook up with others who share your concerns for water quality, and learn about land-use planning issues that affect local waters.

Join a water-quality monitoring organization. If you are concerned about the quality of a nearby waterway or coastal area, hook up with an existing water-monitoring group and find out how it can help you get started.

For Helping to Protect Coastal Wildlife

Support a local wildlife-conservation organization. Also, consider volunteering: Many of these organizations rely on volunteers for staff support and for getting the message about their work out into the community.

For More Information

Plenty of information has been published on the subject of how each of us can contribute to cleaner waters. In coastal states, an excellent source of this type of information is the local Sea Grant office (see "Resources"). Or contact your local Cooperative Extension Service, the public outreach arm of land-grant universities.

The following organizations distribute valuable, detailed information on ecologically safe household management. Many offer recipes for nontoxic household products.

NEW YORK SEA GRANT EXTENSION PROGRAM/LONG ISLAND SOUND STUDY
125 Nassau Hall
SUNY at Stony Brook
Stony Brook, NY 11794-5002
(516) 632-8730

E.P.A. LONG ISLAND SOUND OFFICE
Stamford Government Center
888 Washington Boulevard
Stamford, CT 06904-2125
(203) 977-1541

THE ALLIANCE FOR THE CHESAPEAKE BAY, INC.
6600 York Road
Baltimore, MD 21212
(410) 377-6270
    or:
THE CHESAPEAKE REGIONAL INFORMATION SERVICE (CRIS)
(800) 662-CRIS

The Alliance for the Chesapeake Bay, Inc., publishes *Bayscapes*, an excellent series of fact sheets on environmentally sound gardening, and *Baybook: A Guide to Reducing Water Pollution at Home.*

UNIVERSITY OF CONNECTICUT COOPERATIVE EXTENSION SYSTEM
Sea Grant
43 Marne Street
Hamden, CT 06514
(203) 789-7865

This office publishes *Living with an Eye on Water Quality,* a series of fact sheets about how to integrate water-quality protection into simple, everyday actions.

FRIENDS OF THE SAN FRANCISCO ESTUARY
P.O. Box 791
Oakland, CA 94604
(510) 286-0769

This organization publishes *Estuarywise,* a twenty-four-page booklet made up of one hundred tips for preventing pollution.

An excellent source of environmentally safe household products is:

SEVENTH GENERATION
49 Hercules Drive
Colchester, VT 05446-1672
(800) 456-1177

For information on what boaters can do to be environmentally friendly, write for a booklet called "Water Watch," published by the National Marine Manufacturers Association:

NMMA'S WATER WATCH
200 East Randolph Street
Suite 5100
Chicago, IL 60601
(312) 946-6200

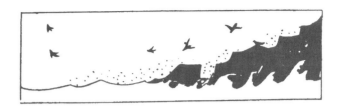

Resources

GENERAL INFORMATION

AMERICAN LITTORAL SOCIETY
Sandy Hook
Highlands, NJ 07732
(908) 291-0055

Dedicated to the study and conservation of the marine environment and the littoral (shore) zone, with a focus on protecting wetlands and fish habitat.

AMERICAN OCEANS CAMPAIGN
201 Massachusetts Avenue, NW
Suite C-3
Washington, D.C. 20001
    or:
725 Arizona Avenue
Suite 102
Santa Monica, CA 90401
(800) 8-OCEAN-0

Focuses on protecting coastal waters, estuaries, bays, wetlands, and deep ocean waters, with particular attention to coastal pollution, offshore oil drilling, and the depletion of fish and their habitat.

CENTER FOR MARINE CONSERVATION
1725 DeSales Street, NW
Washington, D.C. 20036
(202) 429-5609

Focuses on eliminating overexploitation of marine wildlife, on protecting marine resources, and on preventing litter and toxins from being leaked and dumped into the oceans.

CLEAN OCEAN ACTION
P.O. Box 505
Highlands, NJ 07732
(908) 872-0111

Dedicated to improving the degraded quality of New York/New Jersey coastal waters.

COAST ALLIANCE
215 Pennsylvania Avenue, SE
Third Floor
Washington, D.C. 20003
(202) 546-9554

A coalition of individuals and organizations dedicated to protecting coastal regions, with a focus on shoreline development and pollution issues.

ENVIRONMENTAL DEFENSE FUND
Public Information
1875 Connecticut Avenue, NW
Washington, D.C. 20009
(202) 387-3500

EDF can provide general information on ocean- and coastal-related subjects such as coral reefs, oil spills, and coastal wildlife.

NATIONAL AUDUBON SOCIETY'S LIVING OCEANS PROGRAM
550 South Bay Avenue
Islip, NY 11751
(516) 859-3032

Aimed at restoring abundant marine wildlife and healthy habitats in the oceans and along the coasts.

NATIONAL SEA GRANT COLLEGE PROGRAM, R-OR1
NOAA
1315 East-West Highway
Silver Spring, MD 20910
(301) 713-2445

A federal program, representing a partnership between academia, government, and industry, that encourages the wise use of marine resources through research and public education. See list of Sea Grant offices below.

NATURAL RESOURCES DEFENSE COUNCIL
40 West 20th Street
New York, NY 10011
(212) 727-2700

NRDC's Water and Coastal Program focuses on pollution prevention, responsible land use to reduce polluted runoff, water conservation, restoration of coastal ecosystems, and oil spill prevention and cleanup.

SEA GRANT OFFICES

The Sea Grant network provides useful marine-related information derived from Sea Grant research, education, and advisory services, covering subjects such as aquaculture, biotechnology, fisheries, water quality, seafood safety, natural coastal processes, and marine policy issues.

ALASKA SEA GRANT
University of Alaska
P.O. Box 755040
Fairbanks, AK 99775-5040
(907) 474-7086

CALIFORNIA SEA GRANT
University of California, San Diego
9500 Gilman Drive
La Jolla, CA 92093
(619) 534-4440

UNIVERSITY OF SOUTHERN
CALIFORNIA SEA GRANT
Hancock Institute for Marine Studies
University Park
Los Angeles, CA 90089-0341
(213) 740-1961

CONNECTICUT SEA GRANT
University of Connecticut
1084 Shennecossett Road
Groton, CT 06340
(860) 445-3457

DELAWARE SEA GRANT
University of Delaware
College of Marine Studies
Robinson Hall, Room 111
Newark, DE 19716
(302) 831-2841

FLORIDA SEA GRANT
University of Florida
Building 803
Gainesville, FL 32611
(904) 392-5870

GEORGIA SEA GRANT
University of Georgia
Ecology Building
Athens, GA 30602
(706) 542-6009

HAWAII SEA GRANT
University of Hawaii
1000 Pope Road, Room 220
Honolulu, HI 96822
(808) 956-7031

ILLINOIS-INDIANA SEA GRANT
Purdue University
1159 Forestry Building
West Lafayette, IN 47907-1159
(317) 494-3593

LOUISIANA SEA GRANT
Louisiana State University
128 Wetland Resources Building
Baton Rouge, LA 70803-7507
(504) 388-6710

MAINE–NEW HAMPSHIRE SEA GRANT
University of Maine
14 Coburn Hall
Orono, ME 04469-0114
(207) 581-1436

MARYLAND SEA GRANT
University of Maryland
0112 Skinner Hall
College Park, MD 20742
(301) 405-6371

MIT SEA GRANT
Massachusetts Institute of Technology
Building E38, Room 330
77 Massachusetts Avenue
Cambridge, MA 02139
(617) 253-7131

WHOI SEA GRANT
Woods Hole Oceanographic
Institution
Coastal Research Lab., #209
Woods Hole, MA 02543
(508) 457-2000, Ext. 2665

MICHIGAN SEA GRANT
University of Michigan
4107 I.S.T. Building
2200 Bonisteel Boulevard
Ann Arbor, MI 48109-2099
(313) 763-1437

MINNESOTA SEA GRANT
University of Minnesota
2305 East 5th Street
Duluth, MN 55812
(218) 726-8106

MISSISSIPPI-ALABAMA SEA GRANT
CONSORTIUM
P.O. Box 7000
Ocean Springs, MS 39564-7000
(601) 875-9341

MAINE–NEW HAMPSHIRE SEA GRANT
University of New Hampshire
Ocean Process Analysis Laboratory
142 Morse Hall
Durham, NH 03824-3517
(603) 862-3505

NEW JERSEY SEA GRANT
New Jersey Marine Science
Consortium
Building No. 22
Ft. Hancock, NJ 07732
(908) 872-1300

NEW YORK SEA GRANT INSTITUTE
State University of New York
115 Nassau Hall
Stony Brook, NY 11794-5001
(516) 632-6905

NORTH CAROLINA SEA GRANT
North Carolina State University
Box 8605
Raleigh, NC 27695-8605
(919) 515-2454

OHIO SEA GRANT
Ohio State University
1541 Research Center
1314 Kinnear Road
Columbus, OH 43212
(614) 292-8949

OREGON SEA GRANT
Oregon State University
Administrative Services
Building-A500G
Corvallis, OR 97331-2131
(503) 737-3396

PUERTO RICO SEA GRANT
University of Puerto Rico
Department of Marine Science
P.O. Box 5000
Mayaquez, PR 00681-5000
(809) 832-3585

RHODE ISLAND SEA GRANT
University of Rhode Island
Marine Resources Building
Narragansett, RI 02882-1197
(401) 792-6800

SOUTH CAROLINA SEA GRANT
CONSORTIUM
287 Meeting Street
Charleston, SC 29401
(803) 727-2078

TEXAS SEA GRANT
Texas A&M University
1716 Briarcrest Drive, Suite 702
Bryan, TX 77802
(409) 845-3854

VIRGINIA SEA GRANT
Virginia Graduate Marine Sciences
Consortium
Madison House
170 Rugby Road
University of Virginia
Charlottesville, VA 22903
(804) 924-5965

WASHINGTON SEA GRANT
University of Washington, HG-30
3716 Brooklyn Avenue, NE
Seattle, WA 98105-6716
(206) 543-6600

WISCONSIN SEA GRANT
University of Wisconsin–Madison
1800 University Avenue
Madison, WI 53705
(608) 262-0905

CANADIAN COASTAL CONSERVATION ORGANIZATIONS

GREAT LAKES UNITED
Buffalo State College
Cassety Hall
1300 Elmwood Avenue
Buffalo, New York 14222
(716) 886-0142

An international coalition of groups and individuals that promotes the conservation and ecology of the Great Lakes.

GEORGIA STRAIT ALLIANCE
201-195 Commercial Street
Nanaimo, BC V9R 5G5
(604) 753-3459

Focuses on protecting, preserving, and restoring the ecological well-being of Georgia Strait and its adjoining waters.

THE MARINE LIFE SANCTUARIES SOCIETY OF BRITISH COLUMBIA
P.O. Box 48299
Bentall Centre
Vancouver, BC V7X 1A1
(604) 929-4131

Works for the establishment of marine protected areas through lobbying and community participation.

GREENPEACE
1726 Commercial Drive
Vancouver, BC V5N 4A3
(604) 253-7701

The Greenpeace Fisheries and Oceans Campaign focuses on the fishing industry as well as marine, estuarine, and in-river fish habitat.

CONSERVATION COALITION OF NEW BRUNSWICK
180 St. John Street
Fredericton, NB E3B 4A9
(506) 458-8747

A nonprofit, citizen-based organization advocating coastal zone management that integrates environmental protection and fishing management.

ATLANTIC COASTAL ACTION PROGRAM (ACAP)
Environment Canada
5th Floor, Queen Square
45 Alderney Drive
Dartmouth, NS B2Y 2N6
(902) 426-2131

Thirteen community-based organizations striving to achieve ecological sustainability in coastal watersheds located throughout the four Atlantic provinces.

Index